SOME PEOPLE

MALLARD DUCK

© NATIONAL WILDLIFE FEDERATION

CONSERVE OUR WILDLIFE

Peterson —

Holiday Greetings

SOME PEOPLE

HAROLD NICOLSON

WITH AN INTRODUCTION
BY NIGEL NICOLSON

ATHENEUM

NEW YORK   1982

Library of Congress Cataloging in Publication Data

Nicolson, Harold George, Sir, 1886–1968.
  Some people.

    1. Characters and characteristics.   I. Title.
PR6027.I4S6   1982   823'.912   82-71254
  ISBN 0-689-70627-8   AACR2

First published in 1927
Manufactured by Fairfield Graphics, Fairfield, Pennsylvania
First Atheneum Paperback Edition

FOR ELIZABETH

INTRODUCTION
BY NIGEL NICOLSON

Some People was described almost from the date of
its first publication in 1927 as a minor classic, because
it invented a new method of autobiography and perfected an idiosyncratic and highly attractive style. It
has already amused three generations, and its wit is
still so fresh that it is likely to amuse half-a-dozen
more, as Boswell amuses us today. But like Boswell,
Some People is more than entertainment. It is a careful self-portrait of an unusual man, and a reflection of
his age. While Boswell had only two main characters,
himself and Johnson, and his method was direct re-
porting, Harold Nicolson had ten, and his method was
semi-fictional. "The idea," as he explained it later to
a friend, "was to put real people in imaginary situations, and imaginary people in real situations." So he
was free to elaborate or amalgamate people whom he
had known to create "types" and through his imagined contacts with these types to explain his own
changing attitudes and the character or *mores* of his
times. For so short a book, one so entertaining and
superficially trivial, *Some People* contains an astonish-
ing number of themes. In effect it is an entire commentary on human behaviour and hence on society itself.

Something must be said of its origins. It was con-
ceived as a diversion, like the flute-playing of Frederick
the Great, elaborated as a joke, and developed, like
Orlando, Virginia Woolf's near-contemporary portrait
of Vita Sackville-West, into something more serious
than either author had first intended, but without
losing anything of the original *jeu d'esprit.* Early in
1924 Harold Nicolson was invited by J. C. Squire,
editor of *The London Mercury,* to contribute an article on any subject he wished. Being very busy in the
Foreign Office, he found no time to write anything
until in July of that year he went on a walking-tour

of the Dolomites with his wife Vita. In the evenings at various inns he amused himself by writing for Squire the essay on Jeanne de Hénaut, the fifth in this book, while Vita wrote for the Hogarth Press her short novel *Seducers in Ecuador*. (It is remarkable that this fortnight's holiday produced, for each of them, their most original work, and that their diaries, which are eloquent about the scenery and their physical exertions, should make no mention of their writing at all).

Squire turned down the essay on the grounds that it was "too personal," and Harold Nicolson cast it without much regret into a drawer. A few months later he looked at it again, thought it might have some merit, and had it privately printed by Leonard and Virginia Woolf at the Hogarth Press as a Christmas card for a few friends. Among the recipients was Duff Cooper. He *begged* Nicolson to write more essays in the same *genre*, and the opportunity came a year later when he was sent to Tehran as Counsellor in the British Legation. On the outward journey through the Mediterranean he wrote a second essay, *Miriam Codd*, ostensibly about an American woman whom he met on board, and added others as a relaxation during his lonely evenings in Tehran. He wrote them lightheartedly and with enviable facility, completing 4,000 words of *Lambert Orme* in a single evening of December 1926, and kept Vita tantalisingly informed by letter of his progress. One sketch, he told her, was to be about her, under the pseudonym Atalanta, and when she mildly protested, he destroyed the manuscript, as he did the manuscripts of all the published essays. He told his publisher, Michael Sadleir, that he was a little ashamed of the book, and Clive Bell that it was idiotic. When the proofs reached him in June 1927, he threatened to cancel publication, but fortunately Vita was with him, at Isfahan, and persuaded him to change his mind.

The instant success of the book with the general public, and even with Bloomsbury, gave him pleasure and surprise. He had discovered, as if by accident, an original way of stating a novel point of view. He had put into the book more of his philosophy than he realised when writing it. His allusive, self-mocking, pictorial style might, after all, be something more than a parody of Lytton Strachey and Max Beerbohm. It was a tone of voice which the recipient of any of his letters, and later his vast radio audience, would immediately recognise as his own.

But his pleasure was spoiled by the comments, spoken or imagined, of his Foreign Office colleagues, some of whom thought it cheap to poke fun at his profession, and that a serious diplomatist should have neither the time nor the inclination to write such trivia while serving his country abroad. Sir William Tyrrell, then head of the Foreign Office, went out of his way to assure Harold that of course *he* didn't mind, thus conveying, not too subtly, the implication that others did. Harold's own father, Lord Carnock, who had been an earlier head of the Service, disapproved of the book until he was told by a member of the Household that the King had been heard laughing over it out loud. The general opinion was that Harold had taken a great risk with his career, and just got away with it. But had he? Colleagues began to search his diplomatic despatches for *Some People* touches, to be wary of him in social contact, and to disparage his ideas on foreign policy, some of which were highly critical of his masters, by suggesting that he was a brilliant man gone astray, excitable, head-in-air, conceited, disloyal and a little mad. Ambassadors would beg the Foreign Office not to send Harold to their Embassies, fearing his ridicule. This reputation for frivolity pursued him from diplomacy, which he abandoned in 1930 in mid-career, into politics, which he ardently embraced from 1931 to 1948. *Some People* became his trademark. To the day of his death he would groan inwardly when a stranger opened the conversation with the intended compliment, "I read a thing of yours the other day which much amused me. About Lord Curzon's valet, was it, and something about losing his trousers?" Like other men of genuine wit he suffered from the disability that he was taken for a comedian, and expected to perform in character. In fact he was a man of serious purpose and profound convictions.

James Lees-Milne in his two-volume biography of Harold Nicolson, with the help of the copy of *Some People* which Nicolson annotated for Stuart Preston in 1938, has identified the real people on whom the characters in the book were based. All of them are now forgotten except Ronald Firbank, the model for Lambert Orme, and Henry Wickham Steed who with Dr. D. J. Dillon posed for the composite portrait of Professor Malone. All but one of his main characters were half-fictional; the exception was Jeanne de Hénaut, whose personality and appearance were depicted exactly. Some of the incidents actually occurred; all the others could have. To satisfy curiosity about the most popular of the essays, *Arketall,* and to illustrate the degree of truth he mixed with fantasy in the others, it is worth recording Nicolson's own annotations to it. Lord Curzon did have such a valet who accompanied him to the Lausanne Conference, His name was not Arketall but Chippendale. The portrait of Curzon contains no caricature element. When, for instance, he remarks to the youthful Harold, "You are observing the simple squalor of my bedroom. I can assure you, however, that my wife's apartments are of the most unexampled magnificence," the mature Harold annotated, "Those were his exact words." The discussion with Poincaré in the Quai d'Orsay is labelled, "All this is true." So is the story of Arketall's mislaid bowler hat. The arrival of Mussolini in Lausanne is credited, "This is exactly what happened." So far Harold Nicolson had no need to touch up the facts. However, when we come to the famous scene where Arketall, drunk, dances with an American lady in the delegation's hotel, he is obliged to confess, "This has been rather dolled up. Chippendale did dance with the guests, but Curzon had left by then and never saw him." Finally, "It is true about the trousers."

Fact or fiction, *Some People* is true to what Harold

Nicolson observed of the way people behaved in certain circumstances, and as an observer, a Marginal
Commentator, he was unequalled. Every gesture, man-
nerism, glance, pitch of voice, the clothes they wore,
the objects in their rooms, were clues to their personality and hence to their likely behaviour. Miss
Plimsoll comes alive on the second page before she
has uttered a word: "She wore a red close-fitting dress
buttoned down the bust and a little peaked bonnet."
Madame de Hénaut, "from the faded cretonne of
some discarded sofa of 1879 had made for herself
two gabardines." Curzon makes to the journalists "a
friendly gesture at once welcoming and dismissive."
J. D. Marstock, the schoolboy hero, walked with "a
slight lilt in his gait betraying that he was not unconscious of how much he was observed." And in
The Marquis de Chaumont, "I could not have believed that anything not an egg could have looked so
like an egg as d'Annunzio's head," a sentence which
my mother would often quote to me as typical of the
throw-away comedy of Harold's style.

He was not contemptuous of people. He was simply
amused by how often they unconsciously gave themselves away. He pierced with gimlet perception
through the pretences of which we are all sometimes
guilty, our forlorn hope to be thought more congenial,
more liberated, more cultured than we really are, and
he was endlessly puzzled by the odd quirk in human
nature which leads us to imagine that we will get
away with tricks of conceit, snobbishness and con-
descension which we would instantly recognise and
condemn in someone else. Particularly was he fasci-
nated by two types, the gifted but socially disreputable
like Byron and Swinburne, and the powerful or
would-be powerful. Consider this portrait of his Ambassador, Lord Bognor (actually Sir Percy Loraine,
his Minister in Tehran) , in *Titty:*

"I found him sitting at a large desk covered
with expensive photographs in fine silver frames.
His smile was infinitely agreeable, he offered me

a cigarette; his method of approach was that of
man, I felt, to man. 'I want,' he said, 'to get this
business cut and dried.' It was irksome for me
to assist him in this process of desiccation. I
felt that Bognor did not care for Titty, resenting
that a man of good family and public-school
education should diverge so markedly from the
norm. My eyes wandered idly over the photographs: 'Helène' had written the Grand Duchess
Helène: 'Olga' had written the Grand Duchess
Olga; and M. Beguin de Billecocq, the French
Consul in Scutari, had written 'Billecocq' *tout
court.* 'Oh,' I said finally, 'it was only a rag.' 'I
see,' smiled Bognor, sympathetic and broad-
minded. 'You must,' he added with an Anglo-
English wink, 'consider yourself officially reprimanded.' And then, with a gay note of camaraderie—'and what about a little bridge this eve-·
ning? Oh, I forgot, you don't play. But come
and dine anyhow and I'll get some kindred souls.'
I answered that I was engaged."

This passage illustrates another characteristic of
Some People. Harold Nicolson, for all his self-mockery,
always comes out on top. The reader is left in no
doubt that Lord Bognor was a slightly absurd figure
and his reprimand contemptible because he lacked the
strength of character to make it stick. Each of the
nine stories is given a twist, usually at the end, which
leaves Harold saddened by the frailties of humankind
but wiser for the experience. Marstock's brilliance as
a youth is revealed as tinsel by his maturity. The impressive Professor Malone is three times exposed as a
fraud or pseud. The Marquis de Chaumont turns
down Proust because to acknowledge his friendship
might harm his chances of election to the Jockey
Club, to which he is not in the end elected. Bloomsbury ignored Harold (in the marvellous last section
of *Lambert Orme,* where the "untidy man" was in
fact Maynard Keynes and "the lady" Ottoline Mor-
rell) , but the reader is left with the carefully contrived

impression that Harold had got the better of Bloomsbury. In fact the book is a record of how the pre-
cocious Harold gradually grew up, how he rejected
in turn Empire-worship (Miss Plimsoll), the public-
school spirit (Marstock), self-conscious aestheticism
(Orme), snobbishness (de Chaumont) bland affability (Titty), and arrogance (Malone), finding on the
way other delights like literature, travel, friendship,
work, and what he never specifically mentions, sex.

A modern *Some People* would not have been so
reticent, but Harold Nicolson, let us not forget, was
already 40 in 1927, and over 50 at the outbreak of the
Second War. By birth and temperament an Edwardian, there was a limit to the amount of mould-
breaking he could manage, but he managed a good
deal. His book broke the rules of his class by identi-
fying their hypocrisies, and by so doing gave them the
same sort of masochistic pleasure as Lytton Strachey
had given them in *Eminent Victorians*. It is a candid
portrait of the social and intellectual élite in the first
quarter of the century. It tells the reader just what it
felt like to be at Oxford in 1906, an insubordinate
subordinate of the Foreign Office in 1911, or present
at a Bloomsbury party in 1922. It is social history of
a particularly mordant kind. Is this making *Some
People* sound too solemn? Then it is wrong, for if the
book preaches a moral, it is inadvertent; if it is a
period piece, that is because a well-told story can be
as sharp as a photograph. He wrote the book to amuse
himself and others, and as a commentary on what he
was still learning from the multiple experiences of his
generous life.

CONTENTS

SOME PEOPLE

MISS PLIMSOLL

[*1*]

UNTIL recently, the first thing that I remembered was that railway accident in Southern Russia. Stamped upon my mind was the picture of our train brought to a standstill in the open steppe: a snow-bound horizon glimmering like a large white plate under the stars: the engine in front upwardly belching sparks: the carriage at the back, which was the cause of our stoppage, crackling into little scarlet flames; and myself a supine bundle being lifted down from some great height to many hands stretched up towards me—their fingers flickering, as in a Reinhardt play, to the light and shadow of the conflagration. That picture, so vivid to me and so sincere, became a cherished mental possession: it was labelled "The first thing I remember."

I was disappointed therefore when, on my telling my mother how curiously vivid was this my recollection, I was informed that I had got it all wrong. It was true that on returning from Persia we had travelled across the Russian steppes: it was true that the last carriage had caught fire and that the train had stopped; but the incident had happened in the early afternoon of a warm spring day, and I, who was but eighteen months at the time, had slept on unmoved, sucking subconsciously at an india-rubber comforter, indifferent to adenoids and accidents. This adventure has thus been taken from me; it has become but the first of my illusions. Its place in my memoirs has perforce been filled by the picture of Miss Plimsoll, over a year later, arriving at the railway station at Buda Pesth. She wore a red close-fitting dress buttoned down the bust and a little peaked bonnet. She advanced towards us with an expectant and ingratiating manner. Behind her streamed and swayed an undefined background of black, of violet and of gold. It is this background that has so often puzzled me. For years I assumed that the railway station at Buda Pesth was for some reason painted and striped in these predominant colours. But in 1919 I spent a whole week in that railway station, being attached to General Smuts' mission to Bela Kun. We were not allowed, while the negotiations continued, to enter the town. We did our work, we held our conferences, in the dining-car of our own train. It stood there inside the station—a brown international object straight from Paris. The platform on either side of us was isolated by a cordon of Red guards. From the town outside one could hear bands playing and the occasional scream of a factory siren. Hour after hour I paced those two platforms thinking about Miss Plimsoll and the last time, so many years ago, that I was there. I was puzzled to account for that coloured background which formed so large a constituent in my mental picture. In vain I made inquiries. It was only by chance that I learnt later how on the day of Miss Plimsoll's arrival the station had been draped with black and violet curtains tied with golden cords. The Archduke Rudolph had been found dead in his shooting box at Meyerling. The body was passing through that day on its way either from or to Vienna. My recollection, therefore, was abundantly confirmed. This time I was right.

Miss Plimsoll, on being presented to me, said, "Well, dear, we are going to be *great* friends, aren't we?" I was pleased at this, since by rights Miss Plimsoll didn't belong to me at all. She belonged to my brothers, who were infinitely older. I myself had not yet reached the governess stage, but was in charge of Anna, my dear Anna, who was German and had a sewing-machine and used to eat raw bacon on a green plate. We all came out of the railway station and drove to the Andrassy Strasse where we lived. There was a little garden in front with a terracotta fountain, and surmounting the pediment at the top was a statue of Mercury fashioned in the same material. The sirens of the factories would scream and hoot in the mornings while I was being washed.

[2]

I must admit that the figure of Miss Plimsoll, so vivid to me as at first manifested, becomes thereafter, and for a period of two years, somewhat blurred. There is a gap in my recollections in which I cannot visualise Miss Plimsoll, but can only deduce her. The foreground is occupied by Anna, and when I think back to that period my memory adjusts itself to German—strange Teutonic endearments rise slumberously to the surface like old white fish. I know, however, that Miss Plimsoll was there all the time: she it was, doubtless, who forbade me to suck those little cardboard cigarette-holders which one found so often near the benches in the park: she also, it must have been, who placed a veto on our visits to the Panoptikon. The Panoptikon opened off the Andrassy Strasse—on the left as one went towards Buda: there was a little *guichet* where we took our tickets and then a red curtain beyond which swelled a gulf of darkness punctuated by pairs of phosphorescent eyes. These eyes were, in fact, apertures through which one gazed at stereoscopic views of the Place de l'Opéra or the Drachenfels or the war memorial at Coblenz. My brothers adored the Panoptikon: I said I liked it too; but in fact it filled me with an abiding terror: for me the Panoptikon was hell. I was glad, therefore, when Miss Plimsoll decreed that it was out of bounds: it was, she said, exactly the sort of thing that gave little boys scarlet fever.

No, except from the detached and vivid picture of her arrival, Miss Plimsoll assumes definite outline for me only after we had left Hungary for England. The real Miss Plimsoll, the Miss Plimsoll who became so familiar in the years that followed, first emerges standing outlined against the sky of Kent—standing upright, and still in a close-fitting red dress buttoned on the bust, upon one of the ramparts of Cæsar's Camp at Folkestone. Her hand is raised with the index and middle finger outstretched: her hand in the cold wind from the downs is coloured red and blue like a Brigade tie. "Now," she cries, "now, boys, all together. Eastward Ho! Eastward Ho!" Three shrill obedient voices answer her. "Eastward Ho! Eastward Ho!" Miss Plimsoll gazes out in the direction of Dover. "Once again," she exhorts us, waving her hand, "all together! Eastward Ho! Eastward Ho!" Again we shouted response. The picture of her standing there under the wide and gentle sky is very arresting: it is accompanied in my memory by a feeling-tone of discomfort. Even at the age of five I reacted instinctively against the romantic: Miss Plimsoll at that moment saw herself doubtless as stout Cortes; but I, looking up at her, answering her wild plover cry, felt that Miss Plimsoll was showing off. A few days later we all left for Marseilles, and from there by the Messageries to Athens and Constantinople.

Miss Plimsoll wore dog-skin gloves which smelt faintly of ammonia. It was these gloves which she

clapped across my face when the Greek lady committed suicide on the Acropolis. I saw the Greek lady
standing at the edge of the Chalcotheca while we
were visiting the Wingless Victory near by: I saw
that bonneted, tight-sleeved, tight-bosomed silhouette of the early 'nineties sway somewhat and then
bend at the knees as if about to spring: then suddenly there descended upon me the gloved fingers of
Miss Plimsoll trembling violently. I struggled blind-
folded. And when again I was allowed to look the
Greek lady was no longer there. "Hush, darling,"
said Miss Plimsoll when I expostulated. When we
got to the bottom again, there was a large crowd and
several cabs waiting.

At first Miss Plimsoll did not care for Constantinople. She held her handkerchief to her nose when
walking from our house to the Embassy: she mis-
trusted the food and would gaze silently at her plate
for a moment and then attack it rapidly and with
half-closed eyes. This irritated my father. We were
quick to notice that at this period Miss Plimsoll
grated somewhat upon my father's nerves. She was
always asking whether things were "really safe": this
amused us: it was only when we moved up to Therapia that the Cortes side of Miss Plimsoll again asserted itself. It was then only that she settled down.
It was then also that she started the Hut.

[3]

The summer Embassy at Therapia stood at the
very lip of the Bosphorus with only a narrow quay
between its windows and the water. The garden also
was on the water level, and there were magnolias
and rose-beds and winding gravel paths. Behind this
flat portion jutted a wooded cliff, cork trees, arbutus
and ilex clambering up to the top of the escarpment
and spreading up and out into the downland beyond.
A little path zigzagged painfully up the steep incline

and ended in a clearing above the cliff: from here one could look straight down upon the chimneys of the Embassy, upon the sparkling Bosphorus, and out across to where, between the two headlands, the foam of the Symplegades tumbled around the entrance to the Black Sea. A short sharp bar of indigo marked the ocean's eastern horizon. For Miss Plimsoll it represented the unattained: for me it represented merely the word "horizon"—that lovely and that curious word.

It was here, Miss Plimsoll decided, that we should build the Hut. The brisk enthusiasm which she flung into the project was, I suppose, contagious. There certainly was a period, a short and early period, when I also thought the Hut a good idea. We were to build it ourselves. The planks and beams were taken up there on a donkey, and stacked ready for our use. I rather liked that part, and I stumped along beside the donkey carrying a bamboo whisk and shouting "Houah" and shouting "Hou." But when once the dump was ready the donkey was dismissed. We were, Miss Plimsoll said, pioneers: the forest, so she assured us, was virgin: no early settlers, she insisted, had been provided with beasts of burden. I still think she was wrong on this point: I see no reason why, as settlers, we need have been quite so early as all that, and the result was that day by day we panted up that steep incline carrying in empty petroleum tins such objects as nails and hammers and pots of glue and string. A petroleum tin is not an easy thing to walk with and mine was soon taken away from me. My later task was to carry up and down the large bound volume of the *Boy's Own Paper* which contained "the design." And never once was I allowed to use the saw.

For reasons such as these, my early liking for the Hut changed into displeasure, developed gradually into loathing. The legend none the less persisted that we all three adored the Hut, that we could think of little else. "Now, boys," Miss Plimsoll would cry, "stand to!" She had a fervent feeling for the British Navy, and her words of command tended to assume the nautical rather than the strictly pioneer dialect. "Well, boys," my father would say, "how's that Hut getting on?" It was evident that the older generation regarded that Hut not only as meritorious in itself but as an undreamed-of treat for us. This alone would have sufficed to arouse our enmity. But such is the power of suggestion that the Hut was nearly finished before we were sufficiently courageous or united to go on strike.

The occasion on which we downed tools was a sultry, irritating afternoon in August. We had hoped that it was going to rain, and after luncheon we had eyed with relief the thunder-clouds gathering above the Forest of Belgrade. But by tea-time they had rolled eastwards and we straggled sulkily up the hill, banging the petroleum tins against the tree trunks, being doubtless provokingly noisy and inert. Miss Plimsoll, in spite of her headache, was as brisk as ever. She had convinced herself, somehow, that we were working against time. Her words of command rang out crisp and clipped upon the sultry steaming air. "Now then, boys—sharp now! Out with the measure! Let me see! Three feet eight this way and then two feet eleven across. That's right! Steady now! Steady, boys! There she goes! Fits like a rivet!" We were putting on the roof. The cross-beams had already been fixed, and we had nailed down the planks which gave to the building that neat and pent effect. It remained to cover the planks with tarred linoleum to keep out the rain: a large roll of this stiff and inconvenient substance lay among the bilberry bushes. Miss Plimsoll told us to "lug" it forward into the clearing: we lugged. It was then unrolled and we started to measure it out.

Most of our tools were highly professional, but our measure was not. It took the form of a celluloid bulldog with scarlet eyes, from whose navel protruded a little brass ring attached to a long blue tape-measure.

Unless one kept a tight hold on the end of the tape it would spring back with a sharp whirring sound into the entrails of the dog. The linoleum also had to be held down firmly, as otherwise it started to roll up again. The operation of measuring thus afforded a double opportunity for wilful negligence. We grasped this opportunity. Again and again my brothers allowed the linoleum to roll up suddenly while Miss Plimsoll was outstretched upon its surface; and I for my part had great fun with the bulldog. At first I had been given the tape end to hold, but I had let it go so frequently that the process was reversed. Miss Plimsoll ("Now let me see: one foot nine inches"—whirr!) took the little ring at the end of the tape and I was given the bulldog. If one let go of the dog, however, the effect was even more amusing. It would slither along the surface of the linoleum and come up flick against Miss Plimsoll's fingers. The third time this happened she sat down upon the linoleum and looked at me. "I believe," she said, "you are doing it on purpose." My brothers at the same moment released the end of the linoleum, which also came to rest, in the form of a roll, against Miss Plimsoll's knees. It was a declaration of war: a great silence descended upon us, and the lapping of the Bosphorus rose up from the quay below. She gazed in bewilderment at those three flushed and rebellious faces, those three tousled heads. "We *hate* the Hut," we said to her in unison. Her mouth opened in astonishment, and then she began to cry. She pulled out her handkerchief, and dabbed herself with it: "I think you're all horrid," she sobbed, "and when I had taken such pains to get it all ship-shape." She went on crying for a bit, and then we packed up. We descended to the lower level crushed by a leaden load of remorse. The Hut was finished more or less by the gardeners. And twenty years later, on returning to Constantinople, I discovered the remains of it among the bilberries. The little clearing we had made was overgrown with ilex shoots: the Embassy itself had been burnt to the ground in 1910, but one could still look down upon its charred remains, upon the glitter of the Bosphorus, and out to the short dark horizon of the Black Sea. "I think you're horrid," Miss Plimsoll had sobbed into her handkerchief. The sense of remorse returned to me after twenty years.

[4]

Miss Plimsoll's nose was sharp and pointed like that of Voltaire. It was also extremely sensitive to cold. When the thermometer fell below 60° it turned scarlet: below 50° it assumed a blue tinge with a little white morbid circle at the end; and at 40° it became sniffly and bore a permanent though precarious drop below its pointed tip. I remember with what interest I watched that drop as we drove from the station at Sofia. My parents went in front in the first carriage and Miss Plimsoll and I followed in the brougham. The night was cold and we drove along an endless wind-swept boulevard punctuated by street lamps. With the approach of each successive lamp Miss Plimsoll's pinched little face beside me would first be illumined frontways, and then, as we came opposite the lamp, spring into a sharp little silhouette, at the point of which the drop flashed and trembled like a diamond. Then darkness again sweeping up from behind the brougham, and the excitement of seeing whether, when the next lamp came, the drop would still be there. Throughout that winter, that steely Bulgarian winter, I was persistently irritated by the fluid nature of Miss Plimsoll's nose. Yet such is the force of habituation that it never occurred to me to say (as she so often and so sharply said to me), "Miss Plimsoll, blow your nose." My lessons suffered seriously from my dread lest at any moment my copy-book would be sullied by a splash. The thing got increasingly on my nerves. And yet I said nothing. Oh, those secret and distracting worries which gnaw at children's hearts!

My brothers by then were at school. Miss Plimsoll

had me to herself. I can remember, that first night at Sofia, how she sketched out "a plan of campaign." She was unpacking in her bedroom and I sat by the stove. She moved neatly and rapidly about the room, opening cupboards, peering into drawers—her zest in her own tidiness mingling with that vague sense of being put upon which is the brown aura in which all governesses have their being. "Sums first," she said, placing a celluloid box for hair-pins on the dressing-table; "I always think it a good thing to begin with sums; and then from ten to eleven we must do history. The Kings, you know"—(she paused while she placed upon the mantelpiece a framed photograph of H.M.S. *Agamemnon*. She stepped back to see that it was in the centre) —"of England," she concluded with satisfaction. I sat there silently, beginning to feel that I was not going to care overmuch for Bulgaria. "At eleven we stand down. For half an hour you can play in the garden—and then till lunch we do geography." She was silent for a while, intent upon fixing with drawing-pins a brown holland affair of which the lower pouch contained her brushes, and the upper pockets her hair-combings. "There!" she said. "And in the evening, prep." "In the evening, what, Miss Plimsoll?" "Prep." The word had a menacing ring about it, but I inquired no further. I was convinced by then that I was not going to like Bulgaria at all. It had all been so much easier, so far less rigid, at Constantinople.

I feel that, but for Stanley, that year at Sofia would have been marked by a rupture of relations between Miss Plimsoll and myself. Stanley was my pony, and every afternoon I would go out long rides with Mr. Rennie, who was the Secretary, and Mr. J. D. Bourchier, who was the correspondent of *The Times*. Miss Plimsoll the while, in an astrakhan muff and tippet, would walk briskly in the direction of the Zoological Gardens. We met again at tea, our nerves strengthened by this separation. "Sugar, dear?" "Yes, Miss Plimsoll; two." "No, not two, dear, but you can have one of those dear little cakes."

The hostility latent in our feelings towards each other would not, I think, have reached the surface had it not been for M. Stambuloff's fingers. I am still glad that in this connection I behaved so badly: I suspect also that Miss Plimsoll, when she has a tea-party at Southsea, will to this day recount the incident with gusto. But at the time my action led to serious trouble. M. Stambuloff had been murdered in the street: they had attacked him with yataghans, striking him on the head: he had put his hands up to protect himself, with the result that his fingers were severed and fell upon the pavement. They were picked up by an admirer and given to his wife. After the funeral she put them in a large bottle of methylated spirits and placed the bottle in the window of her dining-room, so that the passers-by could see. I was told of this by Zachary, the *chasseur* of the Legation, and I begged my father to take me to see them. He refused. On the following day I asked Miss Plimsoll to come for a walk. She was pleased at this and we started off briskly, talking about the British Navy. M. Stambuloff's house was near the Club, and as we approached it we saw a little knot of loiterers gazing in at the dining-room window. I steered Miss Plimsoll in the same direction and we came to anchor in front of the window. It was a very large bottle, and the eight fingers floated dimly in it like little pickled cucumbers. Miss Plimsoll took so long to realise what they were that I was able to enjoy myself thoroughly. When at last she did identify the contents of the bottle she gave a little sharp scream like a shot hare, clutched me by the forearm, and dragged me violently away. She called a cab and drove back to the Legation: she began to sob a little on the way, and when she got home she burst into hysterics. I for my part was sent to bed.

The next morning I received a full-dress scolding. I was scolded by my father. I was even scolded by my mother. Miss Plimsoll called me into her bedroom and told me to sit down. She then explained to me that my action had not only been heartless but also disgusting. Things, she said, could never be quite the same for her again: all her life, she said, she would be haunted, yes, *haunted* by those fingers. Did I realise how cruel I had been? I said I was very sorry, I would never, never do it again.

The guilt with which these upbraidings weighted my soul developed, in the weeks that followed, into panic fear. I also became haunted by the fingers of M. Stambuloff. If Miss Plimsoll had desired revenge, she obtained it; and I must confess that she behaved in the crisis which supervened with admirable charity, heaping gentle coals of fire upon my head. Night after night the fingers of M. Stambuloff would appear in my dreams, enormous, clustering—not in the least like cucumbers, having circles of bleeding flesh and shattered bone around their base. I screamed and screamed. They gave me a night-light, but a fly walked round the glass rim and threw upon the walls and ceiling a vast shadow of M. Stambuloff, encircling and violent, moving slowly round the walls towards my bed. The night-light ceased to be a solace and became the very centre of my terrors. And it was then that Miss Plimsoll behaved so admirably by sitting up with me until I fell asleep.

Naturally this produced a reaction: I ceased to oppose Miss Plimsoll: I succumbed to Miss Plimsoll. I promised, poor shattered sycophant, that I also would try for the Navy. I felt instinctively, even then, that there was no profession for which I was more singularly ill-adapted. But I had promised, and for several months I endeavoured loyally to share her zest. She gave me for my birthday a real boatswain's whistle: I would blow the beastly thing, forcing myself to picture a line of naval ratings running obedient and barefooted to my summons: the picture caused me little exaltation; "And oh!" Miss Plimsoll would say, "what a *dear* little middy you will make." Here again my response was somewhat languid. I had been on board the *Polyphemus* once at Fiume. I knew very well that the Navy was not for me.

[5]

In a few months my father was transferred to Morocco. Miss Plimsoll was thrilled at this, having discovered that Tangier was in sight of Gibraltar, and having learnt that we would stop at Gibraltar on the way. We did stop at Gibraltar, and on the second night Miss Plimsoll let me down. I have suffered several humiliations in my life, but no humiliation has equalled in thoroughness the incident which then occurred. We stayed at Government House. I was alarmed to discover that this house was called "The Convent." Convents suggested monks, and monks suggested ghosts: the walls of the several cloisters were decorated with grisaille paintings of battles: huge fierce faces with clenched teeth. We were housed in the guests' wings, a cluster of large rooms on the garden-level joined to the main block by an open colonnade. I begged Miss Plimsoll to sit with me until I went to sleep. The first night all went well. On the second night, however, the call of the White Ensign was too much for Miss Plimsoll. She left me, saying that she must write a letter in her room: this was a lie: she did not go to her room, she went into the garden and along the terrace-bastion, from where she could look down upon the clustered shapes of the Fleet winking red and white at each other in the harbour below. I lay in my large bed, watching the moonlight on the slatted shutters, trying hard to be brave. "Miss Plimsoll!" I called to her. There was no answer. "Miss Plimsoll!" I called again; the silence shouted back at me. I climbed out of bed, and my heart thumped within me. I opened the bedroom door. It gave on the colonnade: the shadows of the arches splashed the opposite wall with large white circles of moonlight: a single palm tree, to my right, rustled furtively: I was quite alone in this silent lunar palace: everybody else had died. I ran barefooted along the colonnade hoping to find Miss Plimsoll's bedroom: I turned a corner: there, about to spring upon me, stood a huge black figure with outstretched hands: he was draped in chains; a long loop of chain hung in the moonlight between his right hand and his left. I turned wildly and fled along the cloisters. A red staircase opened in front of me, a wide red corridor beyond. I screamed as I ran, my nightgown fluttering, my bare feet flashing on the carpet. Another and a larger corridor opened out lit by lamps. I screamed: I screamed. A door was flung wide disclosing a huge dinner-table and people in uniform. My mother rose and ran to meet me. She was followed by Sir Robert Biddulph in a scarlet mess-jacket and medals. I was carried back to bed, and Miss Plimsoll was retrieved from the garden. I woke next morning in a haze of shame. Everybody was very kind. Miss Plimsoll led me gently round the corner and showed me the statue of Lord Heathfield holding the keys of Gibraltar on an enormous chain. "There, dear!" she said. "You see, there was nothing to be frightened of —it's only a statue." My humiliation was complete.

That afternoon we crossed to Tangier. We went on a cruiser called the *Arethusa*. Miss Plimsoll was in a mood of fervent reverence. "Now remember," she said to me, "to salute the quarter-deck." I did not know who the quarter-deck was, but I was ashamed to ask: to make sure I saluted everyone I saw. Miss Plimsoll was too deeply immersed in a religious trance to notice: it was rough in the Straits and they gave me a canvas bucket, into which I was very sick. Miss Plimsoll was annoyed at this. "Now, dear," she said, "this won't do at all." "I'm sorry," I said, "Miss Plimsoll." I think she must have realised by then that my heart was not of oak.

When we arrived at Tangier everybody fired a great many guns. My father landed first, and there were more guns and a lot of shrill whistles and people standing rigidly at the salute. Miss Plimsoll trembled violently. I asked her what was the matter. "Hush, dear!" she said: she also was standing to attention, her little nose raised proudly in the air. I was irritated at this, and in any case I felt aggrieved at not being allowed to go on shore with my father. I refused to salute any more quarter-decks. By the time we got into the launch I had made up my mind. "Miss Plimsoll," I said, "I think after all that I won't go into the Navy." She put her hand quickly upon my knee. "Hush, dear!"

[6]

That was all very well. But she nursed a grievance. "Don't you think, dear," she said a few days later, "that we must be careful, we must be *very* careful, not to become a muff?" It was an unwise remark: Miss Plimsoll, in making it, had committed a tactical, if not a strategical, error. I said, "Which of us do you mean by *we?*" She said, "Well, dear . . ." I was no longer a child. I was nine years old. I determined that Miss Plimsoll should be made to regret her innuendo.

I began by executing feats of daring. I was a nervous child, as the saying goes, but physically at least I was (at that date) brave. There was a stucco cornice which ran under the roof of the Legation and I clambered round it, putting my head into Miss Plimsoll's window and saying, very suddenly, "Halloa!" She didn't like that, and complained to my father. I was told not to clamber round that cornice again. I then discovered that Miss Plimsoll was a timid rider. At Tangier in those days there were no roads and no wheeled vehicles: we went to our tea-parties on donkeys or on mules. I rode a horse. Miss Plimsoll and her parasol sat on a leather saddle-seat upon a large white ass. I did not actually jog her donkey, but I did come up behind it quickly and at a trot. The donkey trotted too. Miss Plimsoll's head and jaw bumped and woggled: "Oh, stop!" she cried, and then again, "Oh, stop!" Naturally the donkey, scenting weakness, had no intention of stopping; and Miss Plimsoll fell.

As a result of this incident I was given extra sums. And then one day, as she briskly entered the schoolroom, I locked the door upon her from outside and flung the key out into the garden. It fell among the arum lilies. I got a panic after half an hour and asked the footman to help me find it. We searched in vain. My father observed us searching. A locksmith was sent for, Miss Plimsoll was released, and I was beaten with a bamboo riding cane. "I think," my father said at luncheon, "that it is high time that boy went to school." My mother, somewhat wistfully, assented. Miss Plimsoll sniffed.

Before she left, however, there occurred the incident of the diary. My mother had forgotten that the first of November was Miss Plimsoll's birthday, and we only remembered just before luncheon. There was no time to purchase one of those nice hand-bags which Miss Plimsoll was known to like. My mother discovered, however, a large quarto manuscript book bound in white vellum with leather tags. It had been bought in Venice for a Visitors' Book, and had never been used. It was presented to Miss Plimsoll, who became ecstatic. "Now," she said, clasping the volume to her flat little bosom, "I really *shall* write a diary."

She loved that book. She crooned over it. And one day she produced from the English shop in the town a paint-brush, a mapping nib, and a bottle of Indian ink. She was adept at calligraphy, and across the top she wrote in old English characters "Edith Plimsoll, Morocco, 1899." Then in the centre of the vellum cover, and in larger and even older English lettering, she sketched out in pencil the word diary. I watched her doing it. She measured each letter with the ruler, and there was a great deal of india-rubber needed, and then she brushed and blew away the filings that the india-rubber had left. Then very carefully she uncorked the Indian ink and began outlining the letters with the paint-brush. Her tongue peeped out

beyond her pale little lips, following, now that careful down-stroke, now that up-stroke, which had to be
more careful still. I myself had noticed, when the design was yet only in its pencil stage, that she had written DAIRY instead of DIARY. But I held my peace.
With a fearful joy I saw the Indian ink descend upon
that premature A, pass on to that belated I. The out-
lines were finished: the brush was carefully wiped:
the mapping pen was dipped (her little finger
crooked) into the Indian ink. The letters were then
cross-hatched. I looked over her shoulder. "But, Miss
Plimsoll," I said, when she had got irretrievably to
the R, "you don't spell diary like that." "Oh . . ."
she exclaimed. "Oh, oh!" At this I snatched the book
from her and danced from the room. I burst into
the Chancery, waving it above my head. "Look!" I
shouted, "this is how Miss Plimsoll spells diary!"
Everybody, including the native clerk, was thoroughly amused. My triumph became positively or-
giac. I danced round the garden shouting "Dairy!
Dairy! Dairy!" All my repressions were suddenly released. As usual Miss Plimsoll dissolved into tears.

[7]

And yet, and yet . . . You see, I watched her pack-
ing up. Her possessions had become so familiar to
me. There was that photograph of H.M.S. *Agamemnon*, to which had since been added a companion
picture of the *Arethusa*. There was a strip of Bulgarian embroidery, a present from Philippopolis, which
would one day come in useful: there were those two
phials of attar of roses which she had purchased out
of her own little blue purse at Constantinople: that
Moorish satchel which she had won as a prize at a
book-tea. In they went, one after the other, and a
layer of tissue-paper hid them successively and eter-
nally from my sight. The pressure of *Abschiedsstim-
mung*, the pressure of remorse, rose in me in ascend-

ing levels. That blue dress she wore for tea-parties, that dove-coloured silk which she wore when she came down to dinner. The Diary. The celluloid box for hair-pins. That brown holland affair in which she kept her brushes and her hair-combings. Her brushes themselves. . . . She bent over her boxes, sniffling —but not with cold. "Miss Plimsoll," I said, "I'm sorry—I really am. . . ." She began to whimper at that, and I left the room and locked myself in the water-closet. I cried there softly: soft enough to indicate manliness and restraint: just loud enough to make certain that people could hear. And a few hours later Miss Plimsoll, tear-stained but brave, was bobbing out in a row-boat towards the steamer in the bay.

Years afterwards I met my successor, the boy to whom Miss Plimsoll had gone after she left Morocco. He was a pimply youth at New College and he played lacrosse. He introduced himself to me and said that he felt he knew me already, he had heard so much about me from his governess, Edith Plimsoll. I was alarmed at this, feeling that my sins had found me out. But no—it was evident that Miss Plimsoll had been loyal and romantic. She had conveyed to him the picture of a manly little boy who would have died sooner than tell a lie: the picture of a boy of infinite enterprise and daring, softened only by that gentleness which mates with British pluck. I was somewhat dazzled by this portrait of myself from five to nine. Really that had been very kind of Miss Plimsoll: the whole affair was very satisfactory.

"Tell me," I asked him, "did she bother you much to go into the Navy?"

"The Navy? Good gracious, no. She was always talking about diplomats."

J. D. MARSTOCK

[1]

I AM not of those who thoroughly disbelieve in British education. I have seen so much of the foreign product that I have come to feel that our school system, if placed on a wider basis, may yet prove best adapted to our national temperament. It is true, of course, that it standardises character and suppresses originality: that it somewhat ruthlessly subordinates the musical to the gymnastic. I am not convinced, however, that this is a bad thing. It provides society with a mass of standardised entities who, although unintelligent, yet do in fact possess τὸ βουλευτικόν: upon the individual the effect is only rarely disastrous. The physically gifted enjoy for a short space of years a prominence of which it would be ungracious to deprive them: nor do I think it unfitting that during the same period the intellectuals should very frequently and brutally be snubbed. True originality will by such measures merely be pruned to greater florescence; and sham originality will, thank God, be suppressed.

I admit, however, that my own mental development was checked by my education for a period of some ten years. But the circumstances were exceptional. My home life was so unusually exciting, my school life so unusually dull, that a gulf was formed between myself and my education which it took me a decade to bridge. On the one hand was Morocco, disturbing and aromatic, with wide nights beside the campfire, the smell of gum-cistus, the rootling of wild boar in the swamp behind the hill, the boom of a warmed Atlantic on a distant beach. And on the other were "The Grange" (Folkestone) and subsequently Wellington College; the smell of varnished wood and Sunlight soap, the smell of linseed oil in the pavilion, the white light of acetylene gas upon a Latin grammar. Between these two, sundering them by four days of seasickness, came "the journey"; the heavy P. & O. seething past the light of Ushant and out into the cold wet loneliness beyond. Thirty-six times during those years did I either cross or recross the Bay of Biscay, and thirty-six times did I lie for three days in my cabin while my brothers tried to revive me with exhortations and cheap Médoc and little bits of cake.

I think also that both my private and my public school were exceptionally rigid and restrictive. At the Grange we were cold and underfed: we were incessantly being bothered to live up to our moral tone, which, so they assured us, was higher than that of any school in England. Mr. Hussey, the Head Master, would speak to us of "high endeavour" and kick us if we made the slightest noise. I was puzzled by all this and spent my time dreaming about things to eat, dreaming about warm rooms, dreaming constantly about Morocco. Mr. Moore, the Latin master, had a pair of skis in his sitting-room; Mr. Harrison, the man who taught sums, had only four fingers on his left hand; Mr. Reece one summer gave me a nectarine. I was not in the least unhappy, only absent-minded: they cursed me for being untidy, for laughing in form, for drawing pictures. And the impression arose in me that neither the games nor the lessons nor the high moral tone were things in which, somehow, the masters expected me to share.

At Wellington it was different: one ceased so completely to be individual, to have any but a corporate identity, that the question scarcely arose whether one might or might not be odd. One was just a name, or rather a number, on the list. The authorities in their desire to deprive us of all occasion for illicit intercourse deprived us of all occasion for any intercourse at all. We were not allowed to consort with boys not in our own house: a house consisted of thirty boys, of whom ten at least were too old and ten too young for friendship; and thus during those four years my training in human relationships was confined to the ten boys who happened more or less to be my contemporaries. In addition, one was deprived of all initiative of action or occupation. The masters took a pride in feeling that not only did they know what any given boy should be doing at that particular moment, but that they knew exactly what the said boy would be doing at 3.30 P.M. six weeks hence. We had thus no privacy and no leisure, there was never open to us the choice between two possible alternatives. I entered Wellington as a puzzled baby and left it as a puzzled child. And the vices which this system was supposed to repress flourished incessantly and universally, losing in their furtive squalor any educative value which they might otherwise have possessed.

I repeat that I was not unhappy. I took everything for granted: I even took for granted the legend that we were all passionately devoted to the school. It seemed natural to me (it still seems natural to me) that being bad at games I should, although head of the house in work, be debarred from all exceptional privileges. I was not, I think, unpopular: I was on excellent terms with all the other boys: at football even I finally evolved a certain prowess by being able, at crucial moments, unerringly to tumble down. I would drop like a shot rabbit in front of an approaching onslaught: "Well played!" Marstock would shout at me: I would rise and rub myself, κύδεϊ γαίων—all aglow. But until I came into direct contact with Dr. Pollock I learnt nothing serious from Wellington; and even then my enlightenment was blurred by the vestiges of my admiration for J. D. Marstock.

[2]

How fortuitous and yet how formative are the admirations which our school life thrusts upon us! With no man have I had less in common than with J. D. Marstock, and yet for years he exercised upon me an influence which, though negative, was intense. How clean he was, how straight, how manly! How proud we were of him, how modest he was about himself! And then those eyes—those frank and honest eyes! "One can see," my tutor said, "that Marstock has never had a mean or nasty thought." It took me six years to realise that Marstock, although stuffed with opinions, had never had a thought at all.

I can visualise him best as he appeared when head of the school, when captain of football. A tall figure, he seemed, in his black and orange jersey striped as a wasp. Upon his carefully oiled hair was stuck a little velvet cap with a gold tassel: he would walk away from the field, his large red hands pendant, a little mud upon his large red knees. He would pause for a moment and speak to a group of lower boys. "Yes, Marstock,—no, Marstock," they would answer, and then he would smile democratically, and walk on—a slight lilt in his gait betraying that he was not unconscious of how much he was observed. Those wide-open eyes that looked life straight, if unseeingly, in the face were fixed in front of him upon that distant clump of wellingtonias, upon the two red towers of the college emerging behind. His cheeks, a little purple in the cold, showed traces of that eczema which

so often accompanies adolescent worth. But it was
not an ugly face. A large and slightly fleshy nose: a
thin mouth: a well-formed chin: a younger and a
plumper Viscount Grey.

Under the great gate he went and across the quad-
rangle. He must first look in upon the Sixth Form
room, a room reserved apparently for prefects, who
were seldom in the Sixth. He sank into a deck-chair
by the fire. The other prefects spoke to him about
conditions in the Blucher dormitory, and the date of
the pancake run. Yes, he would have to tell the Master about the Blucher, and there was no reason why
they should not have the run on Tuesday. And then
out under the great gate again and across through
pine trees to Mr. Kempthorne's house. There on the
floor would be his basin ready for him and a can of
hot water beside it. And he had ordered that seed-
cake. The smell of cocoa met him as he entered the
passage. Seed-cake, and cocoa, and Pears' soap, and
the soft hum of a kettle on the gas: then work for two
hours and then prayers. He would read the roll-call
himself that evening. Oh yes! and afterwards there
was a boy to be caned. The basket-work of his armchair creaked as he leant forward for the towel.

[3]

When I arrived at Wellington, Marstock, who was
my senior by some eighteen months, was already
prominent. He took particular pains with me since,
as he informed me later, I reminded him of a little
cousin who had died of scarlet fever. This painful coincidence earned me his protective affection; and I
for my part was awed and flattered. He thought me a
good little boy with a healthy influence among my
fellows: it was his lack of observation, I suppose, or
his influence from the little cousin, which placed him
under this misapprehension. My behaviour, however,
as distinct from my basic morals, caused him many

hours of puzzled anguish. He ascertained one day that I knew the names of only eight members of the school XV. He made me write them all out a hundred times, and repeat them to him after luncheon. I had forgotten to put in their initials, and had to do it again. And then next summer he discovered that I was equally weak on the subject of the XI. My incapacity for games, or "exercise" as they were called at Wellington, filled him with pained dismay. I liked games, and it was obvious that I tried: I used to flounder about and get in the way and shout very hard to the forwards. There was a system called "passing the ball": it meant that one kicked it to someone in front, warning him by shouting out his name: "Hamilton!" I would yell—but no ball would follow. It would have wriggled off sideways somewhere, and I would pick myself up slowly, conscious that once again I was in disgrace. "But you're absolutely rotten," Marstock would say in saddened protest. A lowering grey sky above the white goal-posts and behind them a bank of wellingtonias. "You're *hopeless,* you simply can't be taught." And then the goal-post and the wellingtonias would swim together in a mist of suppressed tears.

Nor was it games alone which showed Marstock that as a pupil I was unsatisfactory. I see myself in retrospect as the most resigned and normal of little boys, and yet I can recollect his chiding me for being mad. The particular occasion for this outburst, the actual manifestation on my part of paranoia, was an ink-pot shaped in the semblance of the Temple of Vesta at Rome. We were not, and with justice, allowed fountain pens: for some strange reason, ink was not provided in the class-rooms: at the beginning of each term we were given a portable safety ink-pot, a red or blue little affair, with a double lid which pressed hard upon the aperture by dint of a round rubber pad and spring. I used to lose my ink-pots. I used to lose them at the very moment when it was time to rush to school. I had had particular trouble on this score with Mr. Elton, who taught me algebra. He told me that if I forgot again I should be whipped. So that morning when I lost my ink-pot I realised how needful it was to replace it by another.

The boy who had the cubicle next to mine was called Juniper. His real name, I think, was McEuan, but he lived at Juniper House, Guildford. I therefore darted into his room to look for an ink-pot. There was none to be found, but on his table was a small brass model of the Temple of Vesta, which opened at the top. It was an ink-stand rather than an ink-pot, it was clearly liable to slop or spill, but it would do. I proceeded with it up to college, gingerly and yet hurriedly as a man wheeling a barrow on a tight-rope. It served its purpose well enough; it was only on my return, my very inky but equally gingerly return, that I was stopped by Marstock. "What on earth," he said, "are you doing with that?" "It's an ink-stand, Marstock." I held out the Temple of Vesta, down the columns of which the ink had poured in shining runnels. "An ink-stand!" he snorted, "who but you would take an ink-stand up to college? And a model of St. Paul's too! Oh, why, *oh, why* will you persist in being different to other people? I give you up; you simply *refuse* to be the same." He paused and looked at me with real perplexity in those open eyes. *"I think you must be mad,"* he concluded solemnly.

I went to my room determined, at whatever cost, not to surrender to this creeping dementia: I must pull myself together: it was only a question of being careful: if one was terribly careful one could succeed in being exactly the same. My whole energy during the terms that followed was concentrated on achieving uniformity.

[4]

The terms passed. Marstock became head of the house, then captain of the XV, then school prefect and then head of the school. I also had crept upwards and was in the Lower Sixth. But this my own prowess was of no avail to me: I was not even a dormitory prefect: I had not yet attained the privilege of leaving my house-cap in the ante-Chapel: I was contented but obscure. And I still feel that all this was very fitting: I have had my fun since: they haven't. Marstock at this stage was, in spite of his glory, very gracious to me: he had given me up as an athlete, but he felt that none the less the school, the spirit which he had infused into Kempthorne's house, had done me worlds of good. He would come into my room sometimes for tea: he would talk about our prospects against Marlborough: I showed a sycophantic but not an unintelligent interest. "Good God!" he would say, "you *are* a freak, but you're less of a freak than you were." And then during his last term there occurred that awful incident which finally shattered in him all belief that I had come to possess, at bottom, some of the right stuff.

The great event of the summer was the match against Charterhouse. Some years we went to Charterhouse, and some years they came to us. That year it was our turn to receive and combat the visiting team. The afternoon, I remember, was hot but overcast: the warm grey clouds spread widely over the wide playing fields—a sheet of shadowed green below, a sheet above of shadowed grey: and against this background clustered little dots of white—five hundred straw hats, white cricket pads, flannels, the scoring board, the staring face of the pavilion clock, the masters' wives and daughters;—some parents, over there under the trees. Reggie Cooper and I had brought a paper bag of cherries and we sat on the grass together—watching carefully lest the other should exceed his share. Reggie then as now was the most stimulating of companions, and it was for me a stroke of fortune that had brought him to Kempthorne's. We had become inseparable; but at least once a week we ceased for a while to be on speaking terms, for several consecutive hours each would avoid the other with averted eyes. The Charterhouse match, the bag of cherries, coincided with one of our moments of reconciliation: we had not spoken to each other for at least twelve hours: we had therefore a great deal to say. The match dragged on around us as we talked: the little white figures on the wide expanse of green would cross and recross slowly, or make sudden galvanic motions with their arms and thighs: a great silence brooded over earth and sky, broken at intervals by the dry tock of ball on bat, by some sharp and distant voice calling directions, by a sudden rattling wave of clapping and applause. Reggie and I joined in the applause with abstracted fervour: we had no idea in reality of what was happening: we clapped our hands when the others clapped, and when the others cheered, we cheered: the bag was getting emptier and emptier; we had already had two arguments which threatened to be of a heated nature, and finally we embarked on the third.

We had scarcely become immersed in this discussion when we observed a ripple passing up the fringe of boys who lined the field. They were standing up and taking off their hats and then sitting down again. Behind them, causing this jagged and rippling edge in the flat line of recumbent figures, slowly walked a group of five people. There was the Duke of Connaught in a grey top-hat, the Master in his robes, the senior tutor, an equerry, and the head of the school. Marstock, who was not in the eleven, walked behind talking to the equerry, giving him doubtless the name and initials of the boy who was bowling, of that boy over there who had so miraculously caught the ball. Reggie and I were lying at the extreme edge of the field, the edge nearest the college. We stood up as they passed us and took off our hats. We watched them enter the Master's Lodge. "That means," said Reggie, "that it's nearly over. They have gone to have tea." We sat down again and continued our discussion. The college clock struck half-past five— surely the beastly match would soon be finished.

Reggie was describing the most exciting day he had ever had. I had already described to him my own most exciting day, giving a slightly coloured version of an attack by Shereefian troops upon a village in the lower Anjera. We had watched from a neighbour-ing hill: the bullets, in my story, had sung above our heads "like this, sizzz. . . ."; the smoke of the burn-ing village had for a moment obscured our vision of the attacking forces: then suddenly it had blown to the west again and the meadow below was dotted with little writhing figures of the wounded and dying. Reggie had been rather bored by my story, supposing, and unjustly, that it was wholly untrue; impatient also to embark on his own. "It was," he began, "the most beautiful morning that I have ever seen. The sea was absolutely blue, and the snow on the distant Alps glittered in the sun. As our yacht steamed into Nice there was first the excitement of seeing whether we were the largest in the harbour. We landed about eleven . . ." I was rather impressed by Reggie's story, regretting somewhat that my father for his part should have failed to be tremendously rich. Reggie's most exciting day, I remember, ended with a visit to the opera. "It was *Tannhauser*," said Reggie. "Not *Tannhauser*," I remarked, "*Tannhäuser*. I thought everyone knew that."

"No, it's *Tannhauser*."

"It isn't *Tannhauser*. It's *Tannhäuser*. There's a di—there are two dots over the 'a' which makes it 'oi.' "

"You're wrong, as usual. It's *Tannhauser*. After all, you don't do German, and I do."

"But, you silly ass, whoever heard it called *Tann-hauser*? Besides, I know German far better than you do. I learnt it as a kid in Buda Pesth."

"You didn't."

"I did. . . ."

There was a wild burst of cheering from the field in which we joined. People were waving their hats, the little white figures of the players trooped suddenly towards the Pavilion. "It's over," said Reggie, "let's do a bunk." We turned and started to run towards the college. As we approached the Master's Lodge we saw a figure running towards us down the drive. It was Marstock. "Well," he panted when he reached us, "what did they score?" I looked at Reggie: Reggie looked at me. "Well, at least," said Marstock impatiently, "they can't have beaten our 278?" I looked at Reggie: Reggie looked at me. "Well, at least we won?" Marstock shouted. We both got very red. "I think we must have, Marstock, everybody seemed very pleased." He snorted and left us. And that evening we both descended to the boot-room and were caned.

I bear no resentment towards Marstock for exacting this reparation. We had committed an enormity, and it was right that the traditions of the college should be maintained. And then it was so obvious that he was deeply and sincerely distressed. He came to my room after the operation and sat upon the settee. "I can't make it out," he said. "I *wish* I knew what to do." He scarcely spoke to me during the weeks that followed. Speech-day came and he received, as was inevitable, the King's medal. We all cheered wildly: he stood there with his back to us, while Princess Henry of Battenberg handed him his badge of honour. I had a lump in my throat: my admiration for him welled up and stung my eyes. And at the end of the term he called me into his room to say good-bye. He put his hand on my shoulder. "You promise," he said to me, "that during the next year you will *try*." I said I would, Marstock, yes, I really would. I left his room hurriedly and on the verge of tears.

[5]

The next term I was moved into the Upper Sixth.
This meant a small but glorified class-room; the desks
were of a different shape, there was actually a carpet,
there were photographs around the room of the Niké
Apteros and of Mycenæ, there was a large plaster cast
above the mantelpiece of a Centaur struggling with
one of the Lapithæ; there was above all constant and
continuous contact with Dr. Pollock. The Master
hitherto had been for me a remote and rather alarm-
ing mystery; my feelings in regard to him were a mix-
ture of fearful curiosity and religious awe: there was
something emotionally magnificent about him, something theocratic. His tall slim figure billowed in a
silken gown as he glided rapidly through the cloisters, leaving behind a faint but pleasant smell of
hair-wash, an impression of something rich and luxu-
rious and mundane: a striking contrast to the drab
penury of our existence: a touch of the great coloured
world beyond. The other masters cowered visibly at
his approach: they seemed, when standing beside him,
to become moth-eaten and affable and unimportant:
the boys, as he spoke to them in his quick and gentle
voice, were somehow more natural and less afraid.
My worship for him had hitherto been uncoloured
by the richer tone of personal intimacy: the Upper
Sixth became for me a large excitement, a rapid intellectual and above all emotional fermentation. To a
large extent, of course, this expansion was due to the
adjustments of puberty, but its development was has-
tened and controlled by the subtlety and sympathy of
Dr. Pollock. He was so intelligent, he was so human,
he was so gently amused: gradually it dawned upon
me that what had hitherto been merely lessons, were
in fact *my* lessons, bore a distinct personal relation to
myself. The school, my house, the games, my efforts to
become "the same" remained, as before, inevitable

and detached: but the work, the Master, the class-room of the Upper Sixth, became gradually a part of my central consciousness, fused gradually with such secret feelings as my people, and the yearning for Morocco, and the novels of Mr. Anthony Hope, and the smell of pines on summer evenings.

I realise, on looking back, that his methods, for all their subtlety, were perfectly calculated and deliberate. He knew that the system of the school had scored upon our brains a few deep grooves of habit which were in danger of becoming rigid: he set himself to render these grooves more flexible, to create new channels and associations in our minds. For the purposes of scholarship, for the needs, that is, of examinations, the Upper Sixth were entrusted to Mr. Perkins, most exact of Hellenists, most meticulous of scholiasts. Dr. Pollock, for his part, appeared to devote his energies to destroying all the educational convictions which we had hitherto absorbed: he taught us that the mere avoidance of howlers was a means only and not an end: he taught us that the greater proportion of classical literature as it figured in the school curriculum was not only dull but silly: that the really jolly bits were yet to come: he taught us that life was more than scholarship, and literature more than books: he taught us to feel, and even to think, for ourselves. The greed with which I absorbed these lessons was voracious: whatever projects I may have had of becoming an exact scholar were destroyed for ever in the space of a few gay weeks; but if I have since understood in any way the meaning and the purposes of culture, my understanding is due entirely to Dr. Pollock. And I render thanks.

For him indeed the classic letters were more human. He dislocated even the setting in which instruction had been conveyed. We would sprawl on pine-needles in his garden, we would lounge beside the fire on his floor. He would give us coffee, strong and redolent, and granulated sugar and little cakes: the two footmen would appear with the Georgian silver and the Wedgwood cups: the contrast with the scrubbed boards and chipped enamel of our school life spread a sense of Olympic ease and privilege; and in his gentle voice he would read to us some lines from Lucretius, a page of Shelley, a passage in Walter Pater, an article even by Max Beerbohm in the *Saturday Review*.

[6]

The conflict between my admiration of the Master and my admiration of J. D. Marstock was still unrealised. The latter, although now at Magdalen, continued by his remembered example to inspire and direct my daily life at school. I was now a dormitory prefect, and I would give to the younger boys such advice and counsel as Marstock in his time had given to me. I taught them with firm but not ungentle insistence that they must all strive to be alike.

It was only in my last term that a slight doubt assailed me regarding the efficacy and necessity of Marstock's ideals. The flash which then illumined my lowering sky was evoked, indirectly, by Dr. Pollock. The contrast between my two allegiances became a conflict and culminated in an explosion.

It was a Saturday evening, and we were sitting under the pine trees reading the Journey to Brundisium. The Master had pointed out to us how indelicate this story was, how gross, in fact, were the sensibilities of the poet: how, in fact, with acquired success, the fingers of Horace had all become thumbs. It was a stimulating theory, and in the middle of it the footman appeared leading a young man in a brown suit across the lawn. I did not recognise Marstock at first, he seemed to have lost something both in height and colour: the eczema was very bad indeed. The Master greeted him warmly and made him join us. We had gone back to that passage about Virgil refusing to play tennis because he had sore eyes. The

Master closed the book and began to talk of Virgil, of his gawky nervousness, of his shy provincialism, of how much he had disliked being made to write the *Æneid*. Marstock watched him with straight but puzzled eyes. "I *loathe* the *Æneid*," I remarked with sudden conviction. Marstock turned his eyes in my direction: they were not only puzzled but disapproving. "But you're wrong," said Dr. Pollock, and then, in that soft and rapid voice, he began to intone:—

"Tum pater Anchises, lacrimis ingressus obortis . . ."

The warm July sun was slanting through the pine trees. The soft and solemn hexameters rolled onwards.

"Manibus date lilia plenis . . .
His saltem accumulem donis et fungar inani
Munere. . . ."

The Master stopped intoning and leant down towards me. "As a punishment for a pert and unsolicited remark you will learn that passage by heart. Whenever in after life we meet again, I shall ask you to repeat it." I glanced at Marstock: his face wore a contented but reserved expression, such as a guest's face should wear when a spoilt, an intolerable, child receives at last the merited rebuke. I looked up at the Master. He smiled back at me with friendly humour; there was a touch of unusual meaning in his smile and he gave just the slightest side-glance at Marstock, I felt my cheeks flaming as from a sudden emotional shock: was it possible, was it conceivable, that the Master could have had an eye-meet with me behind Marstock's back? Was it possible that Dr. Pollock should have found Marstock, even for a moment, even in a little thing, absurd? I walked back under the stars buoyant with some strange delight of liberation. I did not fully comprehend the nature of this winged exultancy: I thought it came merely from the pleasure of that evening, the warm pine-needles, the coffee-sugar, the beauty of those resonant lines. The rows of windows in Kempthorne's house were ablaze between the wellingtonias: I paused in the shadow of the rhododendrons. Three weeks more and I should be free. It was mere humbug to pretend regret. I should be free, free, free. . . . I looked up at the house which for four years had been my prison. The figure of Marstock seemed to rise from it, to assume gigantic shape, to quiver for a moment and then to fall a crumbling idol among the pines. "Poor old Marstock," I murmured, as I climbed the dark and smelling stairs.

[7]

On leaving Wellington I spent nearly a year in Germany. When I reached Oxford Dr. Pollock had been appointed Bishop of Norwich, and Marstock was already preparing for his final schools. He had failed somehow to be given his football Blue and had therefore concentrated his whole energies on obtaining a first. No one has ever worked as Marstock worked, and in the process his straight and open eyes became emptied of all but a forlorn bewilderment. When the examination approached, he funked it. He would stay on at Oxford and work another year: he would make it a certainty. "You see," he explained, "people never know afterwards whether one gets a good second or a bad first. They merely say— 'he got a first at Oxford,' or 'at Oxford he only got a second.' " So for another year Marstock slaved in his rooms in Beaumont Street and succeeded in obtaining a very creditable third. He then decided to enter the Foreign Office. But here again he thought it wiser to take his time. And thus, when I also on leaving Balliol devoted two years to acquiring foreign tongues, I would find Marstock working away in the various *pensions* which we frequented. I went to

Jeanne de Hénaut—Marstock was there: at Hanover,
Marstock: at Pisa, Marstock again. His mind, in all
those years, had become a trifle rigid; but his affection, the memory of the little cousin who had died
of scarlet fever, was wholly to be depended upon. It
was solid and all of a piece: it was like Portland cement: it was exceedingly difficult either to evade it
or to push it aside. He would come walks with me
among the Tuscan hills and wonder what had happened to J. L. Wallace of the Hopetown, or R. B.
Brinsmead of Toyes. I remember in particular a
summer evening in Paris: we had walked across the
river and looked for books under the arcades of the
Odéon: I had shown him the hotel where Wilde had
died, and we had emerged on the Quay at a moment
when every window in Paris and Montmartre was
flaming back at a low red sun. We leant over the par-
apet and looked at the purple river swirling below
us. The hum of life reached us in the hot air; behind
us was the Quartier Latin, in front those myriad
flaming windows. I showed him the two sphinxes at
the end of the bridge and told him how Wilde in
those last shambling years would tell how that sphinx
there on the right was the only person who returned
his smile. "But why," said Marstock, "the one on the
right? They're both exactly the same!" I was silent
at this, looking into the river and thinking vaguely
of mighty poets in their misery dead. "Do you remember," said Marstock, "how after footer one
would come back to the house and one would brew
and read a book?" I said that I remembered very
well.

It was only when Marstock had failed for the third
time in the Foreign Office examination that he passed
definitely out of my life. Fifteen years went by before
I saw him again. The occasion was a public luncheon
given in honour of the Byron centenary. I was late
for the luncheon and found my place with difficulty.
When it was over we crowded into the ante-room. I
suddenly felt my arm seized from behind.

"Well, I'm blowed," said Marstock, "fancy meeting *you* here!" I did not myself feel that my attendance at that luncheon was in any way a startling coincidence, but I forbore to say so. I was pleased to see Marstock again, pleased to notice how slightly he had changed. There was a touch of grey about the carefully combed hair, he was a little thinner, and his eyes had given up being merely open and had become just blank. But it was the same good old Marstock in his brown suit and old Wellingtonian tie.

I asked him what he was doing now. He said that he was an underwriter at Lloyd's. I asked him whether he was married. He laughed a little shyly. "No," he said; "you see it's the wimskies." I put on a serious and condoling expression, imagining that he had mentioned some obscure disease. "The wimskies?" I inquired considerately. "The women, you know—I always call them that. They're all so fascinating, I can't make up my mind." I assured him that, to my mind also, women were delightful and perplexing little things.

I have not seen Marstock since, except once on the Embankment when I passed him in a taxi. But that Byron luncheon is memorable to me for yet another and far more emotional encounter. The crowd had parted suddenly, and in front of me, sitting on a sofa, I saw the Bishop of Norwich. My pulses raced suddenly with a return of the old excitement. I went up to him. "Do you remember me?" I said. He looked up and smiled. He remembered me perfectly. He remembered—ah, yes—"Tum pater Anchises" . . . would I please continue? I hesitated and flushed: not a week had passed during the long years since that evening at Wellington without my repeating to myself those lines, preparing for such an encounter. I knew them perfectly. But for the moment they wouldn't come.

"I am afraid," I stammered, "that I have forgotten."

LAMBERT ORME

[*1*]

IT WOULD be impossible, I feel, to actually be as decadent as Lambert looked. I split the infinitive deliberately, being in the first place no non-split die-hard (oh, the admirable Mr. Fowler!), and desiring secondly to emphasise what was in fact the dominant and immediate consideration which Lambert evoked. I have met many men with wobbly walks, but I have never met a walk more wobbly than that of Lambert Orme. It was more than sinuous, it did more than undulate: it rippled. At each step a wave was started which passed upwards through his body, convexing his buttocks, concaving the small of his back, convexing again his slightly rounded shoulders, and working itself out in a backward swaying of the neck and head. This final movement passed off more rapidly than the initial undulations, with the resulting impression of a face upturned generally, but bowing at rhythmic intervals, as if a tired royalty or a camel slouching heavily along the road to Isfahan. At each inclination the lock of red-gold hair which shrouded the lowness of his brow would flop, and rise again, and then again would flop. He was a tall young man and he would bend his right knee laterally, his right foot resting upon an inward-pointing toe. He had retreating shoulders, a retreating forehead, a retreating waist. The face itself was a curved face, a boneless face, a rather pink face, fleshy about the chin. His eyelashes were fair and fluttering; his lips were full. When he giggled, which he did with nervous frequency, his underlip would come to rest below his upper teeth. He held his cigarette between the index and the middle fingers, keeping them outstretched together with the gesture of a male impersonator puffing at a cigar. His hands, rather damp on their inner side, gave the impression on their outer side of being double-jointed. He dressed simply, wearing an opal pin, and a velours hat tilted angularly. He had a peculiar way of speaking: his sentences came in little splashing pounces; and then from time to time he would hang on to a word as if to steady himself: he would say "Simplytooshattering FOR words," the phrase being a slither with a wild clutch at the banister of "for." He was very shy.

I had not met nor noticed Lambert Orme during my first term at Oxford, but in the Easter vacation he came out to Madrid with a letter of introduction to my people. They asked him to luncheon. I eyed him with sullen disapproval. He stood for none of the things which I had learnt at Wellington. Clearly he was not my sort. He had the impudence to announce that he had resolved to devote himself to art, music and literature. "Before I am twenty-one," he said, "I shall have painted a good picture, written a novel, and composed a waltz." He pronounced it *valse*. My gorge rose within me. I refused during the whole course of luncheon to speak to Lambert Orme. And yet behind my indignation vibrated a little fibre of curiosity. Or was it more than curiosity? I hope that it was something more. Subsequently I was re-

proved by my mother for my behaviour. She said in
the first place that I should have better manners. In
the second place she said that I was little more than
a Philistine. And in the third place she said that she
was sure that poor boy wasn't very strong.

It interests me to recapture my own frame of mind
at the time of this my first meeting with Lambert
Orme. It amuses me to look back upon the block of
intervening years in which I also aped æstheticism,
toyed with the theory that I also could become an
intellectual. Have I returned after all these garish
wanderings to the mood which descended upon me
that afternoon in the dark and damask dining-room
at Madrid? No, I have not returned. It is true that
some faint and tattered fibres of heartiness do still
mingle with my ageing nerves. I *have* my Kipling
side. But I can at least admit to-day that Orme was
in several ways a serious person. And I have been
told by people whose opinion I would not dare to
disregard that such was indeed the case.

[2]

The immediate result of my mother's lecture was
that I promised to take the fellow for a ride. At the
back of my mind (but not I fear so very far at the
back) was a desire to humiliate Lambert, a quite cad-
dish desire on my part to show off. I sent the horses
to the entrance of the Casa de Campo and drove
down there with Lambert in a cab. He mounted his
horse and remained there with surprising firmness,
and, moreover, with an elegance which shamed the
clumsiness of my own arrant style. His languid manner dropped from him; if his back curved slightly it
was but with a Hellenic curve, the forward-seat of
some Panathenaic rider. I was at pains to readjust
my conception of him to this altered angle. We rode
out under the avenues to where the foot-hills look
back to the façade of the palace chalk-white against

the smoke above the town: in front, the ramparts of the Guadarrama were jagged with pinnacles of snow. The larks rose from clumps of broom and lavender: a thousand larks above us: a shrill overtone under the crisp spring sky; and from west to east a flock of April clouds trailed rapidly, pushing in front of them patches of scudding shade. The feeling of that afternoon is now upon me: I see no reason to become sentimental about it: even in our most intimate period Lambert Orme possessed for me no emotional significance: yet I recognise that on that afternoon the sap began to mount within me. That, and the summer evening in Dr. Pollock's garden, are my first two dates.

Not that Lambert said very much. I feel indeed that he was actually unconscious of my existence. He was thinking probably of Albert Samain and of Henri de Régnier, of how pleasant it was, that spring day, among the uplands of Castille. I said: "Over there—you may see it if the sun strikes—is the Escorial." He said, "Yes, I see." I said, "And Aranjuez is over there," pointing vaguely towards Toledo. He turned his head in the direction indicated. "And Segovia?" he asked. I was not very certain about Segovia, but I nodded northwards. "La Granja," I added, "is quite close to it—really only a few miles." We turned our horses, and the wind and sun were behind us. The smoke of the town billowed into sharp layers, an upward layer of white smoke hanging against a sweep of grey smoke, in its turn backed by a crinkled curtain of black. The sun and snow-wind behind us lit and darkened this grisaille. "Oh!" I exclaimed, "what an El Greco sky!" It was an opening. He could have taken it had he wished. He merely said, "Does the King live in the palace? Is he there now?" I answered that he was.

We crossed the Manzanares, where there were women washing white sheets. They beat them against the boulders. The palace above us was turning pink against the sunset. Lambert asked me to tea. I gave

my horse to the groom and walked round with him
to the rooms he had taken near the Opera House. It
was some sort of *pension,* and he had characteris-
tically caused the walls to be distempered with a
light buff wash, and had arranged the room with red
silk, and walnut furniture, and two large gilt can-
delabra from a church. He was very rich. Upon his
writing-table lay a ruled sheet of music-manuscript,
and upon another table some paint-brushes and
tubes of water-colour. He had painted a little picture
of an *infanta* in what I now realise to have been
the manner of Brabazon. It was rather good. There
were a great many cushions and several French
books. He became artificial again when he entered
his rooms and his voice slithered and he ordered tea
in highly irritating French. There was a sheet of vellum lying near the fireplace on which, in an upright
scribble, Lambert had written: "Mon âme est une
infante . . ." and then again "Mon âme est . . ."
and then, very calligraphically, "en robe de parade."
It was cold in his room and he lit the logs in the
fire. He then threw incense on it, and a puff of
scented smoke billowed beyond the grate. My an-
tagonism returned to me.

Lambert thereafter became very foolish about the
tea. He did hostess: his gestures were delicate: there
was a tea-cloth which was obviously his own. I lit my
pipe and said I must be going. He picked up a book
at random: I really believe it was at random. He
said, "Would you like to take this?" I said I would.
It was the *Jardin de Bérénice.* I suppose that, really,
is what dates the occasion.

[*3*]

When I returned to Oxford I visited Lambert in
his rooms at Magdalen, drawn by an attraction
which I should have hesitated to admit. They were
in the new buildings and looked out upon the deer

park: as one sipped one's Malaga, one could hear the stags barking amorously underneath the trees. His sitting-room was exquisitely decorated. When I think of that room I am again convinced that there was something *cabotin* about Lambert Orme: people at the age of twenty should not have rooms like that. He had painted it a shiny black: there were grey sofas with petunia cushions: there was a Coromandel cabinet with the blue china on the top and some hardstone stuff inside. It was not in the least like the room of an undergraduate: it made me at first rather ashamed of my own room with its extracts from "the hundred best pictures," its photograph of the charioteer of Delphi, and its kettle-holder with the Balliol arms: it made me, in the end, like my own room very much indeed. And yet inevitably I was entranced by that little *gîte* (I use the correct word) at Magdalen: by the firelight flickering upon the yellow books: by the Manet reproductions, by the Sobranye cigarettes in their china box. Lambert possessed even in those days a collection of curious literature, and I would sit there after dinner reading *Justine,* or the novels of M. Achille d'Essebac, or even *Under the Hill.* All this, I feel sure, was admirable training. My early oats I find were singularly tame. But they were oats none the less. Lambert at the time was writing his novel *Désiré de St. Aldegonde.* He would read me passages which I failed entirely to understand. They were in the style, curiously enough, of M. Maeterlinck: a style which, in English, tastes like bananas and cream. The book was published some time in 1910 by the Bodley Head. It attracted no attention whatever. And when Lambert, under the influence of M. Guillaume Apollinaire, came to adopt his second manner, he bought up the remaining copies of *Désiré* and burnt them on the rocks at Polperro.

It was all very pleasant and seductive my dropping down like that to Magdalen; but it became a little awkward when Lambert, in his velours hat, would climb the hill to visit me at Balliol. In any case, I never learnt to cope with Balliol until after I had left it: my real Oxford friends were only made when I met them again in after life. The effect of Balliol upon my development was salutary and over-powering. But it didn't work at the time. On looking back at Balliol I realise that during those three years I was wholly abominable. That Balliol should have shared this opinion indicates its admirable sense. But although I had at that time but little conception of what Balliol was thinking, yet I realised quite defi-nitely that they would not, that they did not, ap-prove of Lambert at all. I cannot therefore say that I relished his visits. My sitting-room with its grained wood walls looked somewhat squalid at his entry: the rep sofa, the brass reading lamp with its torn red shade, that other light hanging naked but for a glass reflector: the inadequate books: Stubbs' charters, Smith's classical dictionary, Liddell and Scott—none of that crystalline glitter of those rooms at Magda-len. My scout would burst in with his cap on, and bang the chipped plates beside the fire: the tin cov-ers rattled. The kettle also rattled internally when one poured it out. There was always a little coal inside the kettle. The spout of the tea-pot spouted diagonally owing to a slight abrasion. The cloth was stained and bore in place of embroidery my name in marking ink. There were buttered buns and an-chovy toast. Lambert ate them gingerly.

"I wish," I said to him, being incensed by the re-finement of his attitude, "that you wouldn't wear a hat."

"But if I didn't," he giggled, "I might be taken for an undergraduate."

"But at least not that hat, and at least not at that angle."

"Now don't be tahsome."

There were moments when I hated Lambert. It is a mystery to me how Magdalen tolerated him for so long. The end came, as was inevitable, after a bump supper. I never knew what they did to Lambert: I know only that he escaped in his Daimler never to return. I missed him for a bit, and then I was glad of his departure. I realised that I had been tarred a little by his brush. I mentioned the matter, rather tentatively, to Sligger Urquhart. He seemed to have no particular feeling for Lambert, either for or against: he pouted for a moment, and then said that he had found him "absurdly childish." I do not suppose that that remark was intended to be very penetrating: I know only that it penetrated me like a lance. The angle from which I had begun to regard Lambert Orme was shifted suddenly: it ceased to be an ascending angle and became in the space of a few seconds a descending angle: I had begun, in a way, to look up to Lambert: I now, quite suddenly and in every way, found myself looking down. A few days later Sligger, most subtle of dons, presented me with a copy of *Marius the Epicurean*. I found it on my table when I came back from the river: there was a note inside saying, "I think you had better read this": and on the fly-leaf he had written "H.N. from F.F.U." By this homœopathic treatment I was quickly cured. And yet this false start, if it was a false start, left me troubled and uncertain. I remained uncertain for several months.

[*4*]

As so often in such cases, my ensuing reaction against the eighteen-nineties took the form of a virulent loathing which I have never since been able to shake off. I am assured by reliable people that it was a serious movement of revolt and liberation: I can see for myself that the *Yellow Book* group were all extremely kind and made jokes which, at the time, were found amusing: I am prepared to respect, but I cannot like them. The whole business is too reminiscent of those puzzled and uncertain months at Oxford. It takes me straight back to that room at Magdalen: "Now listen to this, it's too too wonderful: it's really toomuchfun." I have a sense of many little wheels revolving brightly but devoid of cogs. I have a sense predominantly of the early Lambert Orme.

I did not see him again for some five years. He went round the world and sent me a postcard from Yokohama. He was immensely impressed by the beauty of American cities, and it was from them, I think, that he first learnt to see life as a system of correlated planes. It was several years, however, before his very real and original talent for association was able finally to cast the slough of symbolism. When I next met him he was still intensively concerned with the relation between things and himself: it was only in his final period that he became predominantly interested in the relation of things towards each other. His talent, which though singularly receptive was not very muscular, had failed to extract any interesting synthesis from the confrontation of the universe with his own twitching heart: he had tried, and he had failed, to interpret conscious cognition by a single simple emotion. But in his later period he did in fact succeed in conveying an original analysis, implicit rather than expressed, of the diversity and interrelation of external phenomena: he was able to suggest a mood of subconscious perplexity sensitive to unapparent affinities. The conception of life as a repetition of self-contained and finite entities can be integrated only by the pressure of a compelling imagination: Lambert's imagination though mobile was not compelling: I suspect indeed that less power is required to disintegrate such entities, to suggest a world of atoms fortuitously whirling into certain shapes, to indicate a tremendous unknown, quivering below the crust of our convention. His later poetry succeeded because

of its influence to this unapparent reality. I am now
assured that some of his later poems were very re-
spectable.

Meanwhile, however, Lambert Orme continued to
represent for me something "absurdly childish"; his
attitude of mind struck me as undeveloped and out
of date. He was obsessed by false claims. He was no
longer, not in any sense, a guide: he was just someone who rather uninterestingly had wandered off.
The circumstances of our meeting, five years after
he had escaped from Magdalen, confirmed me in this
opinion. It made me very angry with Lambert Orme,
and when I think of it to-day I become angry again.

He came to Constantinople on his way back from
Egypt. He left a note saying that he had "descended"
at the Pera Palace and would like to see me. I was
interested to hear from him again, and told him to
come to the Embassy at 9.30 the next morning and I
would take him sailing up the Bosphorus. I had a
sailing-boat in those days, a perilous little affair,
which I called the *Elkovan*. I had bought it in a moment of optimism, imagining that I would sail daily
out into the Marmora, and that on Sundays I would
go for longer expeditions to Ismid and Eregli and the
Gulf of Cyzikos. But in practice the thing became a
bore. The current which streamed out from the
Black Sea permitted no such liberty of movement. I
ascertained that if I followed the current I should
be unable, when the wind fell at sunset, to return.
So I would tack painfully against the stream, gaining
but a mile or so in as many hours, and then I would
swing round and float back rapidly while the mina-
rets showed their black pencils against the setting
sun. This pastime became monotonous; it was only
on those rare occasions when the south wind blew
strongly that one derived the impression of sailing
at all. The Sunday on which I had invited Lambert
Orme to accompany me was one of these occasions.
A spring day opened before me, enlivened by warm
gusts of the Bithynian wind—the wind which the

Byzantines to this day call νότος: I ordered a large and excellent luncheon; with luck we should get out beyond Kavak and into the Black Sea. We might bathe even. I looked forward to my day with pleasure.

I waited for Lambert Orme. At 10.0 a man brought me a note in his neat Hellenic writing. "To-day is too wonderful," he wrote, "it is the most wonderful day that ever happened: it would be too much for me: let us keep to-day as something marvellous that did not occur." I dashed furiously round to his hotel, but he had already left with his courier to visit the churches. I scribbled "Silly ass" on my card and left it for him. I then sailed up the Bosphorus indignant and alone. When I returned my servant met me with a grin: my sitting-room was banked with Madonna lilies. "C'est un monsieur," he said, "qui vous a apporté tout ça." "Quel monsieur?" "Un monsieur qui porte le chapeau de travers."

[5]

I thereafter and for many years dismissed Lambert from my mind. As a person he really did not seem worth the bother, as an intellect he was absurdly childish—he represented the rotted rose-leaves of the *Yellow Book*. I came to be more and more ashamed of the period when I also had dabbled in æstheticism, a feeling of nausea came over me when I thought of the Malaga and cigarettes in that expensive room at Magdalen. Lambert represented a lapse.

I do not to-day regard him as a lapse. He was inconvenient doubtless and did me external harm. But he represented my first contact with the literary mind. I see now that my untutored self required some such stimulant: that it should have been Grand Marnier and not some decent brandy is immaterial: he provided an impetus at the very moment when the wheels hesitated to revolve. Balliol was all very well, and Sligger Urquhart at least understood and assisted, but my palate was, in fact, too insensitive for so matured a vintage. I therefore look on Lambert, in retrospect, as a short cut. What I failed to realise was the possibility that Lambert also might grow up. His later method, that obtuse angle from which he came to regard life, would, had I realised it, have been an even shorter cut and to more interesting objectives. But once I had discarded him, I did so with no reservations. I thought that any resumption of his influence would entail a retrogression: I failed in my stupidity to see that he had once again sprung ahead of me: and while I dabbled in Bakst and Flecker, Lambert had already reached the van.

As I write of this period, its atmosphere of diffident uncertainty descends upon me. I wish to convey some sharp outline of Lambert Orme, but it all results in a fuzz of words. I am still quite unaware whether I regard Lambert as ridiculous, as tragic, or as something legendary. A section of me is prepared to take him seriously, to read with admiration those of his poems which I am told are good. Another, and less reputable section, wishes to deride Lambert, to hold him up to obloquy. And yet another section feels rather soppy about him, simply because he died in the War. Which is, of course, absurd. Physically he is definite enough. I can see him again, as at our next meeting, sinuously descending the steps of the National Gallery. A day in late October with the cement around the fountains glistening from the damp of fog. A stream of traffic past Morley's Hotel, another stream past the shop of Mr. Dent, a river of traffic down Whitehall. And in the centre, that ungainly polygon, doves and urchins and orange-peel, and a sense of uncloistered quiet. It was the autumn of 1913: he had abandoned his velours, which since our Oxford days had become the head-gear of the proletariate: he wore instead a black Borsalino which he had purchased while studying baroque at Ancona.

But still he wilted: he wilted when I accosted him: he entered the Café Royal with a peculiarly self-conscious undulation which made me shy.

He still employed the old vocabulary (he said that I had been "very tahsome" at Constantinople), but his whole angle had shifted. The former avid subjectivity was leaving him, he was far less excited: his interest in life was no less passionate but had come under some form of control: predominantly he was interested in the sort of things that had never interested him before. He was in love with the wife of the Rumanian Military Attaché at Brussels. He talked about it quite simply as if he had always been a sensualist. He had decided to live in Paris, and had, in fact, already bought a house at Neuilly: he would write and collect pictures, and see to his own education: once a month he would go to Brussels for love and inspiration. He had evolved a not uninteresting theory of the necessity of living in a mechanical framework: at Neuilly the externals of his life were to be organised according to the strictest time-table: every day was in all material respects to be identical with every other day: this rhythmic repetition would in the end produce a background of symmetry against which all new experience would acquire a more intense significance, would assume the proportions of a physical displacement. The eighteen-nineties and the nineteen-hundreds (he spoke of them in a detached and objective manner) had failed because they dissipated their emotions: they were unable either to concentrate or to select. Their system of life was garish and dispersed: his own system, out at Neuilly, would be a monochrome and concentric: he would limit his emotions: he would achieve a pattern rather than an arabesque. I suggested that so artificial a system of detachment might in itself be limiting. He was unexpectedly sensible about it all: he said that he realised that his system could only be an experiment, that even if successful it might be suitable only for himself. But he was

quite determined. And ten months later, in July of
1914, he published *Lay Figures,* which, with his book
of war poems, places him in a perfectly definite position. There is something very mean in me which re-
sents this position. I am not myself very convinced
by it. But it is recognised by people whose judgment
I am honestly quite unable to ignore.

[6]

At moments, in the roar and rattle of the early
stages of the War, I would reflect a little grimly on
the collapse of Lambert's symmetry, on those cobweb
time-tables swept aside unnoticed in the onrush of
the maddened beast. He sent me a copy of *Lay Figures* which reached me in the early days of August
and which remained unopened for many years. Until the spring of 1916 he stayed at Paris, justifying
his existence by a little hospital-work, writing those
poems which figure as "mes hôpitaux" in his war
volume. And then in March he crossed over to England and joined the army. He came to see me before
he left for France. He did not look as odd in his uniform as I had expected: he talked voraciously about
the new movements in French literature and in a way
which I failed entirely to understand: of his training
down at Salisbury he said little, giggling feebly when
I asked him about it, telling me "not to be morbid"
when I pressed for details. I could see no signs of
any alteration in his physique: a little fatter in the
face, perhaps, a little more fleshy round the jaw; but
he still wilted, and his walk was as self-conscious as
ever. I asked him if he was afraid of Flanders,
whether the prospect of the trenches alarmed him as
much as it alarmed me. He said that he dreaded the
rats, and was afraid of mines. "You see," he said, "it
is the evitable or the wholly unexpected that is hor-
rible. The rest is largely mechanical. It becomes a

question of masochism. I certainly shall not mind the
rest." I thought at the time he was being optimistic,
but I have since met a man in the Anglo-Persian Oil
Company who was with Lambert both in France and
Mesopotamia. "Oh no," this man said to me, "he
was a quiet sort of fellow, Orme. And he had a violent temper. But he was rather a good regimental officer: he put up a good show, I remember, at Sheikh
Sa'ad. A very good show. We liked him on the
whole."

Sheikh Sa'ad and Magdalen, that Coromandel
cabinet, those bleached and ochre flats—Lambert
himself would have savoured these contrasts: it was
the sort of thing by which his rather dulled sense of
humour would have been aroused. Was it aroused, I
wondered, as he lay in the hospital ship at Basrah
dying of dysentery? I like to think that it may perhaps have been aroused. He had dignity and courage: I expect he giggled slightly when they told him
that he was unlikely to survive.

I heard of his death as I was running, late from
luncheon, down the Duke of York's Steps. I met a
man coming up the steps who had been at Oxford
with us. "You have heard," he said, "that Orme has
died in Mesopotamia?" I walked on towards the Foreign Office feeling very unheroic, very small. I had
no sense, at the moment, of wastage—that sorrow
which oppresses us to-day when we think back upon
the War. I had no sense of pity even, feeling, as I
have said, that so startling an incongruity would
have illumined Lambert's courage with a spasm of
amusement. I merely felt exhausted by this further
appeal to the emotions: a sense of blank despair that
such announcements should have ceased to evoke any
creditable emotional response: a sense of the injus-
tice of my sheltered lot: a sense of numbed dissatis-
faction: a revolting sense of relief that it hadn't been
me.

[7]

In the summer of 1925 I went to a party in Bloomsbury. I went with much diffidence, alarmed at entering the Areopagus of British culture. They treated me with distant but not unfriendly courtesy. The fact that, through no fault of my own, I was in evening dress increased the gulf between us. I sidled to the back of the room, hoping to remain unobserved. There was a curious picture on the wall which I studied attentively, trying to extract some meaning from its doubtless significant contours. My host came up to me. "What," I asked, "is that supposed to represent?" Had I been less unstrung I should not, of course, have asked that question. My host winced slightly and moved away. I turned towards the bookshelves, searching in vain for the friendly bindings of one of mine own books. They were all talking about a sculptor called Brancousi. I pulled out a copy of Hugh Faussett's *Tennyson* and began to read. An untidy man came up to me and glanced over my shoulder. He had eyes of great kindness and penetration, and he adopted towards me a manner which suggested that I either had said, or was about to say, something extremely interesting. I asked him whether he had read the book and he answered that he had, and that he felt it was so far more intelligent than the other one that had been published simultaneously. I agreed that it was, it was. He then moved away, and I put the book back tidily in its place. On the shelf above it were some volumes of poetry, and among them Lambert Orme's *Lay Figures* which I had never read. I opened it with suddenly awakened interest, and began to turn the pages. My eye was arrested by a heading: "Constantinople: April 1912." I sat down on the floor at that, and began to read. "Thera," I read:

"Thera, if it indeed be you
That are Santorin,
There wander in
The furtive steamers of the Khedivial Mail
    Company,
Rusted, barnacled.
And from the bridge the second officer
Shouts demotic to the Company's agent
Bobbing alpaca in a shore boat.

Thera, if it indeed be you,
That are Santorin,
You will fully understand
This my cleansing—
At which he leant forward and pulled a
    rope towards him,
And the yacht sidled cross-ways,
At an angle,
'That,' he said (he was a man of obtuse
    sensibilities),
'Is Bebek.' "

It went on like this through several stanzas, and conveyed in its final effect a not unconvincing picture
of the poet sailing somewhat absent-mindedly up the
Bosphorus in a little white boat, accompanied, as he
so often repeated, by a man of obtuse sensibilities. I
was a little wounded by this posthumous revelation,
and put the book down for a moment while I
thought. After all, I thought, Lambert didn't come.
If he had come he mightn't have found me in the
least obtuse. I should never have said "That is
Bebek." I should have waited till he asked. And
surely, coming back at sunset, and I so silent—
surely if he *had* come, the poem would have been a
little less personal. My host was searching in the
bookcase behind me, and the rest of the room were
in suspense about something, evidently waiting for
him to illustrate his discourse. "I know," he said, "it's

here somewhere—I was only reading it last night. They want to do a new edition of both books to-gether—both *Lay Figures* and the *War Poems*." I held the book up to him and he took it from me, a little curtly perhaps, anxious to regain his seat and to continue the discussion. "You see," he continued, "there is no doubt that Orme was a real pioneer in his way. Of course his stuff was crude enough and he had little sense of balance. But take this, for in-stance——" He began to turn the pages. "Yes. Here it is. Now this is written in 1912. It describes him sailing up the river at Constantinople with some lo-cal bore: there's really something in it. There really is." At this he adjusted the light behind him, jerked himself back into his cushion, and began. "Thera," he began,

> "Thera, if it indeed be you
> That are Santorin . . ."

He read the whole poem, and when it was finished they made him read it again. They then discussed the thing with appreciation, but with that avoidance of superlatives which so distinguishes their culture. The untidy man leant forward and knocked his pipe against the grate. "Yes, there is no doubt," he said, "that Orme, had he lived, would have been impor-tant. It is a pity in a way. He must have been an interesting man. Did you ever meet him?" He was addressing my host: he was not addressing me.

"No," my host answered; "he lived in Paris, I be-lieve. I've never met anyone who knew him."

The lady whom, from a distance, I had so much admired was sitting in the chair in front of me. She turned round and, for the first time, spoke to me. "Mr. Nicholls," she said, "would you mind opening one of the windows? It is getting hot in here."

I did as I was told.

THE MARQUIS DE CHAUMONT

[1]

I AM now haunted by a companion picture to Lambert Orme—the picture of Jacques de Chaumont. It is a mistake doubtless to place these two in juxtaposition, nor have I any right to suppose that others share my interest in the freaks of literary temperament. And yet Orme and de Chaumont complete each other as a piece of buhl is completed by a piece of counterbuhl. It would be a pity to separate them. Lambert began so foolishly and ended on such a note of seriousness: de Chaumont possessed such possibilities but became in the end idiotic beyond the realm of comprehension. His story, fortunately, will not be believed: but I give it none the less.

The Europeans, during the heyday of King Edward's reign, crowded to Oxford. They founded a dining club which they called "The Cosmopolitan." On alternate Saturdays they would meet for dinner at the Clarendon. The food came from Gunter's and the wines from France. One was expected to get drunk but not disgustingly drunk; and afterwards one played roulette for stakes far larger than I could possibly afford. I was passing at the time through my snobbish period, a phase which in its acute form lasted till 1911, whereafter it became endemic merely, and of late, I feel, but epidemic. At the time, however, I was deeply impressed by the Cosmopolitan. I was excited by their historic names, their Sholte dinner-jackets with the emerald facings, their Cartier watches, their Fabergé cigarette cases, their faint smell of Chypre and Corona cigars; by the fact that they were all far older and more mundane than myself. The Bullingdon, of course, was the Bullingdon; but the Cosmopolitan had a slightly illicit flavour about it: I took to it hesitatingly as a Newnham girl takes to crème de menthe.

The President of the club, if I remember rightly, was Talleyrand-Périgord. The outstanding members were Orloff, and Appony, and Econoumo and Andrea Buoncompagni, and Argenti, and Enrico Visconti Venosta, and Louis René de Gramont, and Goluchowski, and Schweinitz, and the Marquis de Chaumont. I was introduced to the latter by de Gramont, who, since he was at Balliol, was the one I knew best. De Chaumont, even at that date, was an intellectual. De Gramont was not.

I remember particularly one gala evening on which was celebrated the anniversary of the club's foundation. It must have been their only anniversary, since shortly afterwards Talleyrand, who was a German subject and as such a Rhodes Scholar, was sent away owing to flippant behaviour: for which, on arrival in Berlin, he had his ears boxed by his Emperor in front of the whole Court. Appony also left, and so did de Gramont. Visconti went and lived in a little cottage at Iffley, where he studied Bergson: de Chaumont returned to Paris: the club was dissolved. But meanwhile, one warm evening towards the end of May, they celebrated their anniversary dinner. They had by then got bored with the Clarendon, and the dinner for some odd reason took place in the East Gate Hotel. I went as the guest of de Gramont: I sat between him and Enrico Visconti. The Marquis de Chaumont sat opposite. The general conversation was carried on in varying forms of English: the particular conversations were conducted in every language under the sun.

I felt a little self-conscious at first and ungainly: an unpleasant feeling that I did not properly belong. At such moments one realises one's own identity as something physically detached. I saw myself sitting there, my rather scrubby dinner-jacket, my rather wispy black tie, those two inadequate studs, that pink and bumptious face, that curly hair and nose: that voice of mine—surely there was something very unlike me about my voice? And what would Balliol say? I was, and still am, extremely sensitive to Balliol opinion. I felt somehow that the Cosmopolitan did not stand for the things that Balliol stood for: I felt that what the Balliol people criticised in me was exactly that lax strand which had led me to dinner that evening at the East Gate Hotel: as I looked and listened I felt that, for the purposes of Empire, Balliol was right every time: I felt ashamed and apprehensive. After all, it would be rather ghastly if I were seen.

The conversation by then was becoming animated: people were beginning to drink toasts and throw strawberries across the table. De Gramont rose and went and sat next Appony: de Chaumont rose and took the thus vacant chair beside me. He was a pale young man, with straight fair hair brushed backwards, and little red lips, wet and mobile. He suffered from an affection of the eyes, which watered a good deal and fringed his eyelids with a slight inflammation. He had learnt English from his nurse and spoke it fluently with a strong cockney accent. He was, at the time, engaged in studying English literature: he was at the moment rather drunk.

"I 'ave discovered," he said, "the foinest loines in English literature."

"There are many fine lines in English literature."

"No, but these are really admirable. You know them doubtless? They are by Percy Shelley:

"Toime loike a dom of many-coloured glass . . ."

"It isn't 'dom,' " I interrupted, "it's dome."

"Toime like a dome . . ." he began again in a shrill recitative.

I changed the subject. "Where," I said to him, "did you learn English?" It was then that he told me about the nurse: it was then that I told him about the cockney accent. "You mean," he said, "a vulgar accent, un accent du peuple?" I said that that had in fact been my meaning. He became thoughtful at this and drank some more champagne. He then continued the conversation in French. He told me about Madame de Noailles, he recited with great fervour one of the Eblouissements. He was still reciting when, arm in arm, we walked up the High Street. In front of us reeled the other members of the club, their diamonds and their green facings flashing gaudily under the arc-lights. They sang a song in German. I tried to loiter a little behind. I observed two undergraduates leave the pavement at their approach and stand to watch them in disgusted amazement. They were still staring as de Chaumont passed them spouting Madame de Noailles, holding me firmly and affectionately by the arm. One of the undergraduates was Laurence Jones, the other was Julian Grenfell. They observed me. "For God's sake," I whispered to de Chaumont, "do shut up." He paid no attention.

We had roulette afterwards in Talleyrand's rooms above the Bullingdon. De Chaumont stopped playing roulette and sat in the window-seat, looking out upon the warm and gentle night. I went and sat beside him. "Isn't it marrvellous?" he said. "You mustn't say marrvellous, you must say marvellous." An hour later we walked back together along the Turl. "Isn't it mauvellous?" he kept repeating, "isn't it mauvellous?"

[2]

In the few weeks which remained of that, his last, term at Oxford, I saw a great deal of Jacques de Chaumont. He would drop into my rooms in the evening exquisitely although simply dressed, and would speak to me at length and not without ardour of the more obscure tendencies in modern French literature. I was not fully aware at the time of the conflict which must even then have been apparent between the two directing forces of his life, a conflict which in the years that followed played havoc with his happiness and ended, in circumstances which will subsequently be related, by robbing him of a first-class chance of immortality. I realised, of course, that he had a sincere passion for literature, and that he was at the same time particularly sensitive to the advantages, such as they are, of family and position. I did not foresee, however, that his snobbishness would become as a bloated moth fretting the garment of his intellect, that the blue particles in his blood would wage eternal warfare on the red corpuscles with which, in spite of his anodyne appearance, he was unquestionably endowed. I observed, it is true, that considerations of high life assumed for him an importance which appeared, even to me, a little exaggerated. But I did not realise that these same considerations could in any circumstances become an acute mental torment, destroying his intellect as those of others have been sapped by drink, or drugs, or perversion. Yet so it was. His ancestry, his parents, his collaterals loomed in front of him in vast and menacing proportions: the side-streets in his mind were tortuous and quite interesting, but they were interrupted at frequent intervals by rigid avenues leading him back, and so inevitably, to the rue de Varennes.

I can recollect, in the light of subsequent experience, certain symptoms which show me that his disease had already fastened upon him at the age of twenty-two. They had told him, a little unkindly perhaps, that the most exclusive club in England was not, as he had heard, the Royal Yacht Squadron but the equally Royal Automobile Club in Pall Mall. He had thereupon pulled endless strings to secure election to this institution: he had gone up to London and paid a round of calls as if seeking for admission to the Académie Française: when his efforts were crowned by triumphant success, he had some new cards printed with "Royal Automobile Club" in the bottom left-hand corner.

I can recall also a conversation which startled me at the time. Although he concentrated upon all that was best in the University life around him, yet there were moments when his watery eyes would turn northwards a little wistfully, to Blenheim, or southwards, a little wistfully, to Wytham Abbey. We dined at the latter house one evening, and it was in the dog-cart returning under heavy star-twinkling trees that the conversation took place which now recurs to me. I had been saying how much, how very much, I liked Lady Abingdon.

"Is she smart?" de Chaumont asked me.

I was taken aback by this, and asked him what he meant exactly.

"Is she worldly, I mean?"

I assured him that Lady Abingdon was one of the most unworldly women I had ever known. He was silent for some time and when he spoke again it was about Mr. Walter Pater. When I got to bed I realised that by "worldly" he had meant "mondaine."

The foretaste of his final failure, of his final rejection of immortality (a rejection which interests me exceedingly and which forms the climax of this story), was given me some ten months later at Florence. I had spent February, March and April living with an Italian family at Siena in conditions of great discomfort and unremitting study. I would work the whole day without ceasing (I was making up for the time which I had lost but assuredly not wasted at Balliol), and after dinner I would walk through those narrow streets, past the incessant scream of cinema-bells, past the idling Tuscan aristocracy, and out by the great gate into the sudden hush of the surrounding hills. I would walk in this way round the looming walls, entering by another gate, stepping in again among the lights and jingle of the town. It had been a regular, a lonely and an exacting three months: I felt I deserved some relaxation: I went for four days to Florence to stay with Enrico Visconti. He lived in a villa on the hill where there was a huge and scented bath-room and fireflies flickering in and out among the orange tubs. It was very hot, and I was a little depressed by the blatant perfection of the whole business, by the pressure of my one-and-twenty years. Visconti was charming to me and told me a great deal about Bergson and Benedetto Croce which I might not otherwise have known. And one afternoon he took me to tea with a lady, a Countess d'Orsay, who lived on the ground floor of a house on the Lung' Arno. The windows of her drawing-room were shuttered against the evening sun: it was quite dark in the room, a vague impression of people sitting in groups, of red damask and of an almost overpowering smell of narcissus. I was introduced to my hostess, and very shortly afterwards the door opened and in came de Chaumont, a very grey Homburg, and some very suède gloves, in his hand. He did not see me at first, because he was coming from the light into the dark: my own eyes by then were becoming adjusted to the obscurity and I said, "Halloa, Jacques!" He was not displeased to see me and said, " 'Ow are you? What a surprise!"

We sat down behind a red damask screen: Visconti, de Chaumont and myself. At the farther end of the room, behind the smell of narcissus, was a group of Italians talking to each other in the shadows. De Chaumont began to ask me about Siena, and then went on to talk at length, but not without ardour, about Italian literature. I told him that I liked d'Annunzio's early poems. He said that he liked them too: did I know the sonnet which began *"Convalescente di squisiti mali"*? I said I did. Did I know the sonnet which began *"Anche a me l'oro come a Benvenuto"*? I said I didn't. He began to recite it. I thought that this, for a foreigner in an Italian house, was a rather bumptious thing to do. But he continued. He did it rather well. A hush descended on that darkened drawing-room and I became unpleasantly aware that the Italians over there were listening. De Chaumont finished—declaiming the last triumphant line with great courage and distinction. A voice—a woman's voice?—no, a man's voice, a voice like a silver bell, broke in upon us from the corner of the room. The sonnet was being repeated by someone else and with an intonation of the utmost beauty. I leant back in the large red sofa revelling in the languors of that lovely voice, in the amazing finish of that lovely sonnet. There was a hush when he had finished. Visconti whispered to me, "It's d'Annunzio himself." I was too excited to be sorry for de Chaumont.

D'Annunzio then recited some further poems, and notably that splendid metrical achievement called "the rain among the pines." I was enthralled. I crouched back among the cushions, conscious of an emotional pressure such as I had not as yet experienced. He finished and refused to recite again. The sun, as it illumined the green slits of the shutters, had turned to red. Our hostess went to them and flung them open: the room was lightened. I could now see d'Annunzio sitting there playing with an agate paper-knife. I could not have believed that anything not an egg could have looked so like an egg as d'Annunzio's head. He was not very polite either to me or to de Chaumont. I wished rather that he had remained a voice in the dark.

We left eventually and walked along the quay. I was still fervent with excitement. I felt somehow that de Chaumont was unresponsive. I supposed that he was mortified by what had indeed been an unexpected humiliation. I did not press for an explanation. But that evening, sitting on the terrace after dinner, I realised that his reserve arose from more curious and recondite feelings. D'Annunzio, to his mind, was not a man of family: in fact his name wasn't d'Annunzio at all, it was something else. He asked Visconti whether he knew the real name. Visconti couldn't remember. "E un nome," he said, "che fa ridere." I said that it was Gaetano something. Visconti said he thought it was Gaetano Rapagnetta.

"Mais dans tous les cas," commented de Chaumont decisively, "c'es un garçon qu'on ne peut pas voir."

Visconti, who was older than either of us, was much amused at this, and laughed a great deal.

[3]

It was several years before I again met Jacques de Chaumont. In the interval he had published two volumes of his poems and gained thereby a not inconsiderable reputation. I thought his verses good myself and I enjoyed reading them. They were of the pre-war type of French poetry; at the top of each poem there was an epigraph from Laforgue or Rimbaud or Oscar Wilde, and at the bottom a date and the names of such places as Clarens, Coombe-Warren, Halberstadt or Pérouse. The stage-properties which enlivened his later work, the aquariums, cocktail shakers and the Otis elevators, had not as yet disclosed themselves to his Muse; these two early vol-

umes were all about his own extreme and ardent
youth, about greyhounds and gladioli in the manner
of Madame de Noailles. The second of the two volumes, moreover, contained some translations from
Hafiz and a rather empty sonnet to Nijinsky.

I wrote to him about his poetry, and in return he
sent me a large photograph of himself inscribed in a
handwriting that had certainly grown larger since
the Oxford days. "A Harold Nicolson," he wrote,
"cette image sage comme une image. Jacques de
Chaumont." The photograph showed him in a smart
felt hat lighting his pipe and looking upwards, as he
did so, at the photographer. It was an expensive sort
of portrait and it arrived in a fawn-coloured port-
folio with silk ribbons and the name of the shop em-
bossed in gold. But in spite of that there was
something a little equivocal about it, something
which I felt could not have been wholly welcome in
the rue de Varennes. It may have been the pipe, or
the hat, or that upward expression. "Jacques," I
thought, "is becoming Bohemian." But that was nonsense. I looked at it again. No, there was nothing at
all Bohemian about that photograph.

He published a third volume of poetry contain-
ing a sort of Pierrot masque which was very dull indeed. I heard that the book had fallen flat; and
shortly afterwards I heard that de Chaumont was
coming out to Constantinople in Madame de
Béthune's yacht. There were seven people on that
yacht, and by the time they reached the Bosphorus
they had got considerably on each other's nerves.
My chief, who was a friend of Madame de Béthune,
gave a large banquet for her the night after her arrival. He invited all the Young Turks to meet her.
There was Enver in his neat little uniform, his hands
resting patiently upon his sword-hilt, his little hair-
dresser face perked patiently above his Prussian collar. There was Djemal, his white teeth flashing
tigerish against his black beard: there was Talaat
with his large gipsy eyes and his russet gipsy cheeks:

there was little Djavid who spoke French fluently
and who hopped about, being polite. (It is odd,
when I think of it, how many of my acquaintances
have been murdered, how many have been hanged.)
We waited over half an hour for the Béthune party,
and then the Ambassador told me that I must rearrange the dinner, as he could wait no longer. I was
annoyed at this, since when seven people drop out
of a dinner of thirty-five it is difficult at short notice
to rearrange the places. I went into the wide corridor outside the drawing-room and began rather
sulkily to draw plans upon a sheet of foolscap. The
Ambassador, an impatient man for all his charm and
brilliance, came out and told me to hurry up. I resumed my task feverishly and in despair; a sound of
voices reached me from the central court below: I
dashed aside my pencil and my paper with relief;
they were all squabbling together as they came up
the staircase. De Chaumont came last.

I put him next to myself at dinner, thinking he
would be pleased by this attention. He was not
pleased. His eyes wandered watering around the
table with an expression which no trained diplomatist can fail to recognise. He was thinking that he
should have been accorded a higher place. I explained that I had put him next to myself on purpose.

"That's roight," he said, "and Oi'm jolly well
pleased to see you."

I felt that he might have said that before. We
talked for a bit about old times. We then spoke of
his poetry. It was a little awkward for me about that
last volume which, as I have said, had fallen flat. I
remarked that I had thought it a very delicate piece
of work, which was strictly true. He was rather bitter about the whole business. "You see," he said,
"were Oi Monsieur Jacques Duval Oi should not be
exposed to these hattacks. But as it is, the Jews, the
Freemasons, and the Socialists controive to insult me.
Moy own people of course object to moy publishing,

at least in moy own name. Oi assure you that it is very difficult for someone with a name like moine to be taken seriously." I suggested that both Lamartine and Chateaubriand had triumphed over similar difficulties. He smiled at me pityingly and murmured something about country squires; "Ces hobereaux," he said. I realised how wide a gulf must be fixed between La Nouvelle Revue Française and the rue de Varennes.

The next day he came to luncheon with me: we were to spend the afternoon in the bazaars. I asked Pierre de Lacretelle to come with us. It was not a successful arrangement, since Jacques insisted on talking English and Lacretelle as the day wore on became visibly annoyed. I must confess that de Chaumont on that occasion proved maddeningly superior. He arrived in a yachting cap and very white flannel trousers. He talked the whole time about people who were completely unknown to Lacretelle or myself. And he went on and on about how difficult it was for a man of family to succeed in literature. I asked him why, in such cruel circumstances, he did not change his name. He was evidently shocked by this suggestion and scarcely disguised the fact that he considered my remark ill-bred. "Soyons sérieux," he remarked as we entered the blue galleries of the bazaar.

Lacretelle, I fear, behaved rather badly. He urged de Chaumont to purchase the ugliest and most expensive objects that could be found. And he kept on saying that it was a mistake to visit the bazaars in a yachting cap as it made people raise their prices: besides, they might guess who de Chaumont really was. We said good-bye to him, a little coolly, at Galata bridge. It was then that Lacretelle exploded. He said that there were only two types of men whom he really detested. The first were the *gratins* and the second the *rastas*. De Chaumont by some strange alchemy combined both these qualities. "Et en outre," he continued, "il exagère. On n'est pas snob à ce point-là. Et remarquez-le bien, c'est un fat. Il fait des bouts rimés qu'il appelle des vers: il achète des descentes de lit qu'il appelle des tapis."

During the few days that the yacht remained at Constantinople, I avoided asking Lacretelle a second time to meet de Chaumont. I suggested to the latter that rather than endure the conflict between his breeding and his writing, he had better decide firmly to sacrifice the one or the other. It didn't much matter which he did. He agreed that the problem was one which imposed itself. I suggested that he might consult Madame de Béthune, who was a woman of judgment and intelligence.

"Une femme remarquable," he assented, "une femme remarquable. Mais américaine, américaine. . . ."

[*4*]

It was Lacretelle's indignation, rather than anything that he had said or done himself, which opened my eyes to the defective in Jacques de Chaumont. At Oxford his intellectualism had detached itself as something vivid and sincere. I had taken it for granted that de Chaumont's passion for literature was the unquenchable fire of his being, and I did not consider it possible that such a flame could fizzle out under the cold water of the rue de Varennes. It did fizzle out. It is possible, of course, that had he lived in the *grand siècle* his two dominant inspirations might have mingled in the production of respectably sincere poetry: had it not been for the War he might even have produced some decent work in the manner of Henri de Régnier. But the War drove the gentle muse of second-rate poetry away from the colonnades and gardens and made her walk the streets. In one volume, his last volume, de Chaumont accompanied her, and there was a great deal about asphalt and the lovely legs of the Eiffel Tower and the beauties of reinforced concrete: his muse walked the pavements with the others, but she wore goloshes and was terribly afraid of being recognised: so that his fourth volume, as his third, was a failure. The promise of his juvenilia had not been fulfilled: he proclaimed that literature had gone to the Jews and Socialists: he returned to the fold of his collaterals: he read nothing except the Action Française: he began to think of marriage: he had long discussions with the Abbé Munier: he ceased even to get his clothes in London: he bought a pair of yellow dogskin gloves.

When I met him again in 1919 the effects of this degeneration were sadly apparent. He had spent the greater part of the War on the staff of General Lyautey in Morocco. On his return to Paris he was rapidly demobilised. Even as Rimbaud before him, he repudiated not only literature but his literary friends. I saw him at Foyot's, where I was dining with Lacretelle and Jean Cocteau: he sent me a note by the waiter asking me to lunch with him the next day at the Ritz: he paid no attention to my two companions.

It was with great relish that I was able the next day to tell him what an ass Cocteau had said that he was. He was rather pathetic about it. He almost convinced me that for his futile faubourg flabbiness there was something to be said. He spoke of his mother; a widow: she was getting frail and old: he was an only son: he would not wish to cause her pain. He spoke of his aunt de Maubize, of his uncle the prince, of how in France, under the Third Republic, it was impossible to compromise. "You see," he explained, "there are so few of us. We must keep together. We are the trustees of refoinement and distinction." I knew but little at that time of Parisian conditions and I almost believed him. I merely asked him how such people as the de Beaumonts, or Princess Marie Murat, managed to reconcile their dynastic and racial duties with the enormous fun they got out of life, with the intellectual benefits they conferred on others. He smiled at me a little pityingly, making it clear that I was talking of things which only a very few people were privileged to understand. "It's moy mother," he added again. I had never seen his mother, and he was evidently in no way anxious that I should do so. I pictured her as an aged and a pathetic creature in black lace and diamonds, engrossed in religion, engrossed in Jacques. I know full well how these obligations can grow upon one, how loving hands can stretch out from the older generation to strangle the ardour of the next. How many of my friends had suffered from such infanticide, how many had cramped their style for fear of what Aunt Juliet would say at Little-hampton, or Uncle Roderick at Bath! I felt that I understood de Chaumont's point of view, I felt that on the whole he was behaving rather well.

And then, by chance, I met his mother at lunch-eon.

Jacques, I am glad to say, had not been invited. She was a brisk and manly little woman like a fox-terrier, and she rushed up to me jumping about and firing off little short sharp questions in a series of rapid barks. I was a friend of Jacques? He had often spoken of me. What were we to do about it? Was he in love? Did I think he would marry? Why had he chucked writing? Why had he dropped all his in-teresting friends? Why had he become such a bore? Et snob—enfin? She turned to a woman who was standing beside us. "C'est inconcevable, ma chère, à quel point ce garçon est devenu snob." "Ça doit être le jockey," her friend answered.

Madame de Chaumont agreed that it must be the jockey. They turned to me simultaneously—did I also think that the jockey was the cause of Jacques' inexplicable behaviour? I am not easily shocked, but I admit that at this question I blushed scarlet. I stammered something about his never having told me anything about it. I have since made frequent endeavours to remember exactly the words I used.

I may have said, "He has never spoken to me about
the jockey"; on the other hand, I may have said, "He
has never spoken to me about *a* jockey." When I realised subsequently that they were referring merely
to the Jockey Club, I saw how vast a difference, what
a gulf between correctitude and flagrant indiscretion,
stretched between the use on my part of that definite or that indefinite article. To this day I remain
uncertain which of the two I employed. I remember
only that I was acutely embarrassed and that everybody laughed.

[5]

It was about this time that the Prix Goncourt was
awarded to Proust for *Du côté de chez Swann.* Proust
began to be lionised. He would lie in bed all day in
his stuffy darkened room, and in the evening he
would put on his elaborate evening clothes (those
white-kid gloves clasping an opera hat) and attend
the reception given to the members of the Peace Conference. He appeared there like Beethoven at the
Congress of Vienna. He would flit about looking like
a Goanese bridegroom. He would flit from Mr. Balfour to M. Venizelos, from Marshal Foch to M. Ber-
thelot. He was very friendly, and ill, and amusing.
He enjoyed hearing stories about the Conference.
He seemed quite unaware of the early and enduring
monument of his own impending fame. He drank a
great deal of black coffee and stayed up very late.

On one such occasion he said that he would like
to introduce me to the Marquis de Chaumont. I said
that this was unnecessary since I had known de
Chaumont for many years. He begged me not to be
so unintelligent and so gross. Surely I must realise
the pleasure it gave him to take an Englishman by
the arm, to propel him across the room, to say, "Mon
cher Jacques, permettez . . ." to hesitate and then
to begin again, "Permettez, Monsieur, que je vous

présente mon grand ami le Marquis de Chaumont."
For me it would be perfectly easy. I should only have
to say, "Oh! but I know de Chaumont, we were at
Oxford together." And then the three of us could sit
on that sofa over there and talk about the other
people. "Vous voyez bien," he said, "c'est d'une sim-
plicité. Allons-y! Ne soyez pas inintelligent!" I sur-
rendered myself to this comedy. Proust purred like a
small Siamese cat. De Chaumont, I am glad to say,
was exquisitely polite. We sat on the sofa as arranged. As arranged, we talked about the other people.

After a few minutes de Chaumont rose and left us.
We then talked about de Chaumont. Proust was indignant with me for regretting that so bright a talent should have been ruined by an undue deference
to foreground. He did not agree with me in the least.
He said that there were a great many young men
who could write much better than Jacques de Chaumont, and very few young men who could show so
many quarterings. It was right and fitting that
Jacques should concentrate on the qualities which
he possessed in so highly specialised a manner. The
world was becoming too diverse: it was necessary to
specialise. "Il ne fait que cultiver sa spécialité! Il fait
bien."

"I shall now speak to you," he said, "on the subject of elegance."

I was all attention, but fate cheated me of that
discourse. We were interrupted by our hostess:
Proust rose, and a few minutes later he drifted away.
I leant against the window watching him. A little
white face over there, those bruised eyes, that blue
but shaven chin, those white gloves resting upon the
opera hat. He was being universally affable. I never
saw him again.

I walked away from that party with Jacques de
Chaumont. I told him how excited I was by Proust,
how Antoine Bibesco had promised on the following
Sunday to take me to dinner with him in his

bedroom. De Chaumont was not enthusiastic: "Un homme remarquable, évidemment, un homme remarquable: mais juif, juif." And that dinner never materialised. I have recently seen the letter which Proust wrote on that occasion to Antoine Bibesco. It was a letter in which he begged the latter to come alone on Sunday and not to bring me with him. The letter was quite kindly worded.

[6]

A few weeks later we heard that Proust was again seriously ill. He had been working at *Pastiches et Mélanges*, and the effort had exhausted him. De Chaumont came to see me in obvious tribulation, carrying a letter in his hand. I read the letter. It was from Proust, saying that he had written a short sketch in the manner of St. Simon and would Jacques mind if he figured in it by name? The latter was embarrassed how to answer. He did not wish to offend Proust, yet on the other hand, well, really . . . I said that I, for my part, would have been in the seventh heaven had Proust showed any inclination to insert me in *Pastiches et Mélanges*. De Chaumont said, "It moight be jolly well all roight for a foreigner, but moy mother would not loike it." I told him that I had met his mother, and was convinced that she would not mind in the least. He was only slightly disconcerted. "Then there is moy aunt, de Maubize. She 'ates Jews." I began to get a little angry at this, and told him that I doubted whether Proust would live for long, that he was the greatest living writer, that Jacques was sacrificing a free gift of immortality, and that what on earth could it matter about his aunt? He sat there turning the letter over and over in his gloved hands. Suddenly he tore it up with a gesture of decision: he flung it into one of the large brass bowls that enlivened the foyer of the Majestic.

"Non!" he said, "non pas! Ça me ratera mon Jockey."

The book appeared some months later and it contained no mention of Jacques de Chaumont. And the following year I met a member of the Jockey Club and asked him whether de Chaumont had been elected. He said that he had not been elected.

JEANNE DE HÉNAUT

[1]

THERE was a lake in front of the hotel, cupped among descending pines, and in the middle of the lake a little island, naked but for a tin pagoda, with two blue boats attached to a landing-stage of which the handrail was of brown wood and the supports of pink.

It was this that made me think again of Jeanne de Hénaut.

"Je voudrais," she had announced one evening, "si ma vie était encore à faire, habiter auprès d'un lac."

"Quel lac?" Marstock asked. Jeanne closed contemptuous eyes at him through the brown veil of her own cigarette smoke. She did not care for Marstock: he was not, she felt, quite up to her standard: assuredly he had less intellectual distinction than her other pupils.

"Je voudrais," she began again, "si ma vie était encore à faire . . ."

"Mais ça," said her brother (it was one of the eve-

nings when he took the late train home to Rueil),
"ça, ma sœur, c'est un alexandrin."

"Je dois ajouter," I intervened sententiously, "que
c'est aussi du Verlaine."

"Moi," said Eustace Percy, "je ne goute pas les vers
libres."

"Ni moi non plus," added Marstock with sudden
emphasis.

"Jeanne," mumbled her mother, scratching the
top of her bald brown head with a table fork,
"Jeanne, ce que tu m'embêtes avec tes lacs! Tu as des
idées saugrenues."

As usual Jeanne allowed her mother's interjection
to pass unanswered. The eyes which she had shut
abruptly at Marstock remained ruminant and half-
closed. She rolled another cigarette, running the paper edge along her tongue as if closing a letter card:
she swung the damp, discoloured cigarette before her
with a rotatory gesture as of an acolyte swinging a
censer. I knew what she was thinking about: she was
thinking about gongs, and Cochin China, and (had
she known it) the Lily of Malud, and white jade
opium pipes and how much she disliked Mr. Marstock. But she said nothing of all this. She smoked in
silence for a space of time while her brother told us
a story about how a man in his office had gone off
suddenly to Madagascar.

"Ça serait si calme," commented Jeanne finally.
The incense of her drab and dripping cigarette arose
around her, as might well be at Tonkin, and loitered
slowly-drawn among the black and wiry undulations
of her hair.

[2]

We were never sure, never either absolutely or
unanimously certain, whether it was a wig. On the
one hand there was the parting down the middle, a
brown oleaginous parting, with nothing about it of

that waxen or that canvas effect which one associ-
ates, respectively, with the expensive or the cheap
peruque. On the other hand, there was the texture
of the hair itself, as of the tail of a black stallion,
fiercely symmetrical, undulatable only by the tongs
of Vulcan himself, and framing the square visage
squarely—giving to it the flat and formal contour of
the Queen of Spades. The face itself, the skin of the
face, was uniform in texture: smooth and yet un-
healthy like a large, soft, yellow apple: slightly
soiled and bruised. Her figure was as indefinable as
her sex. She was not a tall woman, and yet sometimes, as when her thoughts veered home to Theodora, Empress of Byzantium, her head would be flung
back and upwards with an imperial gesture that
added to her height. She was not a short woman,
and yet, in her Mandalay moments, or when she was
thinking of Mary Queen of Scots, she could become
dumpy as a jade Buddha, or shrink into her ruff with
a faint suggestion of the *petite;* and on such occasions
her rich baritone voice would flatten instinctively
into the betel-nut accents of the Far East or mince
and narrow into the lip-consonants of the Court of
France. Her clothes were equally personal and de-
ceptive. From the faded cretonne of some discarded
sofa of 1879 she had made for herself two gabardines, beginning under the jaw in a stiff ruff of the
later sixteenth century, and ending around her yellow, ink-stained hands in two little frills, smocked
for an inch or so around the wrists.

Her age was for us a problem of very frequent
discussion. Until the coffee incident occurred we had
but scanty data on which to found our theories.
Jeanne was ever reticent about all but her immediate past. We knew only that as a girl she had lived
at Constantinople, where her father had been in-
structor to the Imperial Ottoman Cavalry: we did
not know, until the coffee incident, the date, or even
the approximate date, of this significant sojourn.
The coffee incident enlightened us: it happened in

this wise. At luncheon every day we had cutlets: they were good cutlets, but we had them every day. It was thus that we looked forward, a little unduly perhaps, perhaps a little greedily, to the coffee which closed our frugal meal. Towards the end of the luncheon the aged Madame de Hénaut would shuffle out to the kitchen in her bedroom slippers and would return with a tin coffee-pot steaming at the spout. On this particular morning Marstock had been very funny, in his own manner (he was a man who avoided paradox), about the fables of M. de Lafontaine. I was slightly annoyed myself, feeling that Marstock, in his indirect English way, had somehow missed the point of Lafontaine's style. Which is good. But upon Jeanne (who did not care for Marstock) the effect of his humour had been more subjective: when her mother returned with the coffee-pot she intimated, a little sharply perhaps, that she, that morning, did not want any coffee.

"Comment, Jeanne," squeaked Madame de Hénaut from the doorway, "alors tu n'aimes pas mon café?"

Jeanne assumed the Theodora manner. She raised a deliberate head and the black eyes glittered imperially. "Vous comprendrez, messieurs," she said, "que quand on a bu le café préparé pour Sa Majesté le Sultan, alors . . ." and this with a wide sweep of the cigarette dismissive of all *ersatz* concoctions. Dismissive also, on that occasion, of our own coffee: for by then her mother had bolted backwards with the coffee-pot and slammed the door behind her, squeaking, "Jeanne, ce que tu m'ennuies avec tes Sultans!"

". . . pour le Sultan," continued Jeanne imperially, and unperturbed, "ce pauvre, cher Sultan. Il s'est suicidé quelques jours après. . . ."

The door opened again suddenly and the brown medlar head of Madame de Hénaut (who had been listening outside) darted through it and hung there with sparse dishevelled locks like some trophy of the

Borneo head-hunters.

". . . et dans *notre* jardin," the old woman added.

"Et dans *notre* jardin," continued Jeanne, the imperial baritone flattening into the minor key of reminiscence, "c'était à Ortakeui: le pavillon de Sa Majesté donnait sur notre jardin. On l'appellait le petit, dit *Kutchuk,* Tchéragan. C'était un beau soir tiède d'Avril. Les arbres de judée entaient en fleur. J'avais à peine seize ans. . . ."

Our attention, which, during Jeanne's *adagio* movement, had been wandering somewhat into vague regrets of coffee, was arrested by this remark. Abdul Hamid, I seemed to remember, perhaps inaccurately, had succeeded as Padishah in the later 'seventies, and his deposed brother had cut his throat soon after. It would have been in '76 or '78. Jeanne, by her own confession, was sixteen at the time. She must, therefore, be about fifty or fifty-three: we put it at fifty-five to be safe.

The security of our deduction was shaken by another incident which occurred a few weeks later. It is tabulated in my memory as the "de Musset incident." For we had been talking about Madame de Polignac and electric light, and M. Jacques Blanche (for Coleridge Kennard had by that time succeeded Marstock), and this led inevitably to Alfred de Musset. Coleridge Kennard said that the man was a bore. I interposed something deprecatory, but at the same time defensive about the plays, and then (for I was at that date beginning to summon up the courage of my convictions) about the *Nuit de Mai.* Coleridge Kennard flickered for a moment with his fair entangled eyelashes and began to talk hastily about the law of diminishing returns. But Jeanne, whose interest had been aroused by the mention of de Musset, quickly assumed the Georges Sand manner, squared her yellow jaw, and pointed with her ink-stained finger (it was green ink) at the little withered, wizened, crouching figure of her mother.

"Ma mère!" she exclaimed peremptorily. It was

as the crack of the showman's lash. Her mother started and ceased suddenly to scratch the bald brown place on the top of her head.

"Moi," she tittered with senile coyishness, "vous n'y croirez pas, messieurs, mais j'ai *dansé* avec Alfred de Musset."

Jeanne, still the ringmaster, surveyed us with triumph. "Figurez-vous, messieurs," she concluded, pointing at her mother as if at some particularly revolting specimen in a medical museum, "*ça,* a dansé avec Alfred de Musset."

"*Avec* Alfred de Musset," repeated her mother, raising a brown hand, withered like the claw of an old hen. "*Avec* Alfred de Musset."

I was sorry then that Marstock had left us. He would, assuredly, have asked, "And what was he like?" As it was, we received the triumphant circular glance of Jeanne with courtesy, with appreciative interest, but in silence. I have an impression that Coleridge Kennard, who was then in his symbolist period, slightly sniffed. Eustace Percy assumed that firm cognisant expression which has subsequently, and how rightly, endeared his personality to the Mother of Parliaments. And I was merely doing sums in my head. Surely, if Madame de Hénaut had danced with de Musset, it must have been before that most under-estimated poet had been cradled by Georges Sand into dipsomania: before, that is, he became incapable of any such gratuitous gyrations: let us say in the year 1834. So that Jeanne, biologically speaking, must be much more than fifty-five.

We all, if I remember rightly, became a little thoughtful that evening.

[3]

The flat which Jeanne shared, in tolerant but ill-masked disdain, with her mother was on the top floor, the fifth floor, of number 174 rue de la Pompe, Paris, XVIe. On the street level there was a glass door, the smell of beeswax, the concierge Madame Stefjane ("Mais elle exagère, cette femme. On ne s'appelle pas ainsi."), and a little lift with the most menacing instructions printed on a card. Coleridge Kennard wrote a prose poem about that lift (it was during his symbolist period), which appeared in the *Westminster Gazette*. It took one up the five stories with a persistent grunt of protest, and, when one had clanged the iron gate and pressed the push marked "descente," it would sink down with a sudden, and rather pointed, exhalation of relief. The same dutiful hostility was noticeable in the manner of Madame Stefjane herself. In front of the door to Jeanne's flat there was a horse-hair mat under which, on the rare occasions on which any of us dared to venture out after 9 P.M., Jeanne would hide the latchkey. "Je mettrai la clef pour vous sous le paillasson," she would say, in the tone of Catherine the Second sending Potemkin on a mission to Vienna. And at 11.45 P.M. the same evening, there the key would be.

But in general one rang the bell. It rang very loudly, and the maid (Eugénie her name was) would open the door somewhat nervously. The first impression was a smell of fish. For Jeanne would buy the discarded fish of the quarter and let it simmer from 1 P.M. till dinner-time, when it was given to her cats. Behind the smell of simmering fish was the flat itself. A little hall in the first place with a Bokhara rug. The kitchen beyond, and opposite to it the dining-room. And then the dark, unlighted passage which swerved to the right round the well of the staircase and formed the backbone of the flat. There was a drawing-room next to the dining-room, into which we never entered: it was used at night as a bedroom by Madame de Hénaut. She slept presumably upon one of the divans which decayed against the wall: in the morning sometimes she could be met emerging from that room in a nightgown and a dirty fur cape, a cigarette in one hand and in the other a round enamelled object of the most domestic significance.

At the period which recurs to me more vividly there were only three of us living and learning at 174 rue de la Pompe. Eustace Percy had the room beyond the *salle à manger*. He would emerge energetically from his books, pass a hurried white hand over a harried white brow and engage in the conversation with force, fluency and distinction. I was, and still am, immensely impressed by Eustace Percy. So was Jeanne. She cherished the idea that one day he would be King of France. "Voilà," she would say, "mon candidat." I imagined for some stretch of time that she meant by this cryptic and so recurrent tribute that he was her favourite for the Foreign Office examination, which indeed was a cert. But she explained to us all one evening that I was wrong: for had not the son of a French duke ascended not so very long ago, if one considered the Palæologi, to the throne of England? "Et en somme il était bâtard, tandis que Lor' Eustache, à ce que je sache . . ." She was a most ambitious woman. She was also a royalist; but one who had to admit that the official candidates to the throne were not very inspiring. So she was obliged to fall back upon compromises such as Eustace Percy, and stamping her letters upside down, and referring generally to the Third Republic as "la grosse Marianne."

Marstock had the room next to Jeanne, between it and the cubicle drawing-room. It opened out of the passage on the left, and was small and tidy. Marstock was large but also tidy. On his mantelpiece he had a set of the English Men of Letters Series which began with those square red ones and ended with those thin yellow ones. "My tutor," Marstock would say, "told me that the examiners expect one to have read the E. M. of L. S." He had a way of abbreviating the classics; he rolled his r's when he spoke French. Jeanne, as I have said, did not care for Mr.

Marstock: "il ne me plaît pas," she would say, "ce goujat." Such a word was unusual with her, and, as such, all the more impressive.

My own room was at the end of the passage, beyond the locked door which was that of Jeanne. Often as I groped for the handle I could hear her talking to her cats. "Cochon," she would hiss at them, "Ramasès, tu n'es qu'un cochon; et toi, Zénobie, tu es pire." But we never saw the cats. The door was locked against us: it was only by the faint smell that hung about the passage, and by the angry scratches upon Jeanne's hands, that we knew where they were housed. She seldom spoke of them. They belonged to that inner life from which we were excluded: to that inner life which was a jumble of theosophy, and Buddhism, and howdahs and punkahs, and chutney, and the repetition to herself of "Om mani padhi om"—all of which she had culled from the excellent encyclopædia of M. Larousse.

My own room, as I have said, was at the end of the passage. From my part of the balcony I could overlook the garage opposite and out beyond the trees of the Bois to the domed height of the Mont Valérien. If I leant forward and looked to the right I could see the pink marble of the Castellane Mansion in the avenue de l'Impératrice (Jeanne called it that to humiliate M. Fallières). If I looked to the left I saw only the narrow cañon of the rue de la Pompe diminishing to a point of perspective. Between the two windows there was a bookcase, and a table below with a crochet cloth: there was also a bed and a red marble mantelpiece with a brass lamp and a papier-mâché tray on which I kept my yellow packets of Maryland. Under the bed was a flat tin bath.

We all, in those days, came to work for a month or so at a time under the enigmatic discipline of Jeanne. One could go to Paris for a bit, and then to Hanover, and then to Siena or St. Sebastian, and then back to Paris. But as French and German were the two most important languages, we tended to spend

most of those preparatory two years either with
Jeanne in Paris or with Lili and Hermine at Hanover. The Foreign Office examination was held in
August of every year, and we inclined generally to
pass the last three months at rue de la Pompe. There
was something in the discipline of the establishment
which aided that last summer sprint: besides, one
could keep up one's German with Herr Schmidt, and
there were Spaniards and Italians also who arrived
at strange hours at 174. It was a strenuous existence.

[*4*]

In the years that have since intervened I have
often endeavoured to recapture and to analyse the
secret of the hypnotic spell which Jeanne was able
to cast upon us. For, after all, we were not children
at that time: we were graduates of the University of
Oxford: we had by then asserted and acquired our
independence; we were, to say the least, of age. But
in the white-heat discharged from Jeanne's convictions, Balliol and Christ Church, Annandale and Bullingdon, became but as the snow upon the desert's
dusty face: within a week we would be assailed by
the furtive submissiveness of a private-school boy:
we would find ourselves throwing bread at each
other when her back was turned: and within a fortnight our scale of values had so altered that we welcomed Jeanne's cloud-capped illusions as our own.
For such is the force of faith, and such the mesmeric
influence of legend; and it was on these two founda-
tions that Jeanne based her system and her power.

The newcomer in this way would, during the period of his novitiate, be subjected to an intensive
course of the great historic legends of the past. There
had been Robert Vansittart: he had written a French
play at the age of sixteen and it had been performed
at the Odéon: he had, after a bare six weeks of
Jeanne, passed first into the Diplomatic Service.

There was Lor' Moore who, beneath an exterior of gentle distinction, concealed a will of iron—"Que dis-je? Une volonté d'acier." There was Mr. Tyrwhitt, who would assuredly have proved an archi-first at the examination had he not, that August, been stricken with ophthalmia; to become thereafter "ce pauvre M. Tyrwhitt, si spirituel, si génial enfin, mais qui avait ses mouches." A later epic was that of Colum Crichton Stuart, who was descended, whatever he might say, from Mary Queen of Scots, and who had smuggled grouse for Jeanne through the Calais customs, and who spoke French in the manner of the late Duc d'Aumale. And finally, and, as it were, contemporaneously, there was "M. le Baron Kennard, qui était d'une élégance, mais *d'une élégance* . . ." and who was the intimate friend of that important but deleterious writer M. Maurice Barrès.

Around these gigantic figures Jeanne would weave her saga; and we, the tyros and the aspirants, would gaze at each other with a vague surmise, wondering whether any of us would be able, would be *worthy*, in our turn, to enter such a pantheon. I realise, on looking back, that Eustace Percy must have attained his apotheosis. I have an uneasy feeling, however, that I myself never figured with any striking prominence in Jeanne's mythology. I have questioned my successors (frank and friendly people like Tommy Lascelles and Alan Parsons, and Charles Lister and Duff Cooper), and they have been obliged in honesty to reveal to me that in the blaze of Eustace Percy's legend my own little star became a trifle dimmed. I cherish no rancour and but little envy in the matter: merely a slight and quite recurrent regret.

Be this as it may, the models of what we should, and after all could, become were kept constantly before us: they had been men fashioned in our shape, leading the lives we led, sitting at the very table that we then surrounded. And now they were gods: nay, more, they were in the Foreign Office. Of course we were impressed: we had never, somehow, seen our-

selves and our impending career from so cosmic an
angle: and with this sudden realisation of our privilege came a fiery sense of responsibility towards ourselves, towards our country, towards Europe, towards
posterity, and predominantly towards Jeanne herself.
Deliberately, she exploited the impression thus cre-
ated: whilst keeping before our eyes the Olympian
heights attained by the successful, she would indicate at moments that for those who did not conform
there was the Malebolge of failure; there was even
the possibility that they might be asked to leave. The
dread of such a disgrace, the fear of the dark and
voiceless limbo into which the unsuccessful were
plunged, fired our nerves and galvanised our muscles into prodigies of endurance. We accepted without a murmur the squalor and the discomfort of our
surroundings. It never occurred to us to protest or
to escape. We would rise at five and drop exhausted
to our beds at midnight: and it was in vain that
around and below us the delights of Paris glittered
to the throb of Circean violins.

The passionate though restrained emotionalism
with which Jeanne flung herself into the task of our
education produced, as I have said, a phenomenal
change of values. We began to share her fakir-like,
her hypnotic, powers of concentration; we also began
to feel that nothing in this life or after was of
any import except the examination: mesmerised by
Jeanne's incantations, by the glittering crystal of her
own conviction, we abandoned to her our will, our
liberty, and our reason. She held us enthralled.

[5]

That there was something mesmeric in Jeanne's
hold upon us occurred to me long afterwards when
I was told by Alan Parsons of the incident of Patrick
Shaw Stewart. For Shaw Stewart, who imagined that
the rue de la Pompe was some sort of *pension*, actu-

ally called there one evening after eleven o'clock and
rang the bell. The door was opened finally by Jeanne
in her dressing-gown: Shaw Stewart asked politely
but firmly if he might see Bunt Goschen: he was
taken grimly along the passage and shown the room
that once was mine. He failed entirely to understand
the enormity of his action: they tried in hushed whis-
pers to explain it to him, but he simply could not
grasp what it was all about: in the end he left in a
huff—slamming the flat door behind him, and leaving the front door open upon the street. Jeanne announced next day that Shaw Stewart's action "l'avait
blessé jusqu'au cœur": and it was months before his
friends could rid themselves of the impression that
the latter had in fact behaved very badly, or that
Jeanne's indignation was not splendidly justifiable.

A similar exercise of hypnotic suggestion centred
around the *"cahier."* This was a notebook in which
were inscribed the most brilliant compositions of her
most brilliant pupils. It was the palladium of the
establishment. To be included in the *"cahier"* became the devouring ambition of us all: in the flare
of that aspiration such University honours as we had,
or had not, attained waned into insignificance. She
kept it in tissue-paper. When one had qualified or almost qualified for inclusion, she would bring it with
her to the morning lesson. She would arrive with her
crocodile-skin writing-case, her travelling clock, and
the little khaki fountain pen with the green ink, and
one's ear would catch with greed and apprehension
the rustle of the tissue paper which enshrined the
"cahier." She would not mention the latter, but put
it down on the chair beside her; and, in general, she
would take it away with her when the hour was over.
But one felt that one had at last been accorded a
glimpse of the Holy Grail.

And then, I suppose, behind the fear and venera-
tion with which she inspired us, there burned a very
real, if at the time unrealised, feeling of pity. For

Jeanne was a lonely woman. Her mother she most cordially disliked. Her brother, whom she adored, was married and had a family, of which she was acutely jealous, out at Rueil. They had no friend except an old Colonel who would come sometimes on Thursdays to visit Madame de Hénaut, until my dog bit him in the leg. At which Jeanne was delighted. They had no relations except a cousin, a certain Major Mangin, who had served in the colonies and who had once given a lecture at the Institut Géographique. He was no more than a vague name to us: he never came to the flat.

Her whole life, her whole existence, was concentrated upon her work. She believed sincerely that God had granted to her the mission to coach young Englishmen for the Diplomatic Service, and her flaming faculty of self-deception had invested this mission with a gigantic import. She was an uneducated woman. The foundation of her learning was the encyclopædia of Larousse. She had at one period been through every word in that dictionary and evolved therefrom a little yellow book in which she analysed (quite inconclusively) the genders of all French substantives. Of literature she knew nothing: "Pour moi," she would announce when the conversation led her into deep waters, "il n'y a que Shakespeare, Dante, Goethe, Racine—et rien d'autre." And there was nothing more to be said. And yet with all this she had an amazing sense of the French language, of the frigidity of the thing and its balance. Her intuitions, at moments, amounted to genius. She knew instinctively just the sort of phrasing and idiom which would convey to the examiners the impression that one possessed "toutes les aisances de la langue française."

And predominantly, perhaps, there was her passionate interest in the examination for which we were working. She could tell one the exact marks which had been obtained in any subject by any given candidate in the last ten years. She believed with an unswerving faith that no one could succeed unless they had been through the mill of the rue de la Pompe. She resolutely ignored the fact that French represented only a tenth of the marks required, or that there were other teachers in other places who could teach, and actually had taught, the language. The brilliant Monsieur Turquet of Scoones she could not absolutely ignore; but she got round him: she recommended to her pupils "une légère couche de Turquet avant de venir ici," by which M. Turquet was relegated to his place. And as for Hanover, or St. Sebastian, or Siena, she conveyed the impression that these were subsidiary establishments vaguely within her empire.

As the date for the examination approached, her excitement (nobly controlled) and her solicitude equalled that of M. Descamps supervising the training of Georges Carpentier. Nothing was omitted that her own ingenuity or the ministration of Larousse's encyclopædia could suggest. She would put large chunks of sulphur in our bath water: I strongly suspected her of mixing *tamar indien* with the soup: she would arrive in the morning with a nectarine on a plate; and in the evening she would ask us to rub little bits of camphor behind our ears. It was Larousse also who suggested to her the expedient, one hot July day, of draping the dining-room window in dripping blankets: the experiment was not a success: the room was completely darkened: the people in the flat below sent up to complain of the cascade which had descended upon them: and Madame de Hénaut became definitely disagreeable: "Ça te dit quelque chose, Jeanne, tout ce tra-la-la? Pour moi ça n'a ni queue ni tête." So the blankets were taken down.

And then, at the end of July, I left for London. As my cab turned the corner of the avenue de l'Impératrice I could see Jeanne upon the balcony in her nightgown waving a bath towel.

[6]

It was not till after the War that I saw her again. I had come to Paris for the Peace Conference and one of my first visits was to the rue de la Pompe. Jeanne received me in the drawing-room. Her mother had died some time in 1915. She had since the War had no pupils. She was looking ill and underfed. In comparison with the old Jeanne she appeared a little shy and uncertain. The former jet-like glitter was gone. As I was leaving I asked her if she had minded the air-raids. She admitted that she had minded them terribly. "But of course," I said, "you could go down to the ground floor—in a tall house like this there cannot have been so great a danger." The eyes flashed for a moment with their old fire: she drew herself up with the old Theodora manner: "Non, monsieur!" she exclaimed in her resonant baritone, "Non, monsieur! La cousine germaine du Général Mangin couche au cinquième."

I did not see her again: she died soon afterwards; and in 1919, meeting General Mangin at a dinner-party I told him about Jeanne and the air-raids, thinking he would be diverted by the story. He was not diverted. He failed, I think, to observe in it anything either of pathos or of humour. He drew himself rigidly to attention. He struck his chest so that all the medals thereon danced like harebells upon the Downs. And then he started shouting. "Ah ça!" he shouted. "Ah ça! C'est bien elle: c'est bien la France!"

On recovering from my astonishment at this outburst, I reflected that, after all, the General might be right.

TITTY

[*1*]

His Christian name was Nevile, his second name, Titmarsh, and his surname that of one of the most ancient and formidable of the Scottish clans. His mother was markedly Spanish, being in fact descended from the Prince of Peace. I had once seen the lady eating an éclair at Rumpelmayer's in the rue de Rivoli—a stout little partridge, covered with frills and Cartier rings, vivacious, petulant, and bearing about her the fading glamour of the Edwardian period. She wore black buttoned boots, very tight and small, with which she drummed on the rubber floor. Titty was disliked by his mother, who, I fear, regarded him as a shameful and inconvenient little appanage. With his father, a remote and solitary laird somewhere in Inverness, his relations were very strained indeed. His mother, at recurrent intervals, tolerated Titty and would allow him to visit her at Beaulieu. His father never tolerated Titty, who was but seldom allowed to come to Inverness. This parental indifference dated from the time when Nevile had been a wizened, rather mean little boy at Miss Pincoff's seminary at Folkestone; his parents at that period had not yet separated, but his mother rented a house of her own in South Street, where she would give luncheon-parties to the leaders of Edwardian Society. Titty did not attend these parties.

I met him first at St. Petersburg, where I had gone for my Christmas holidays. My people were dining out the night I arrived and had instructed him, as being the junior of the secretaries, to be my host for the evening. Titty was bilingual by origin and possessed in addition a curious facility for modern languages: he had thus passed young into the Diplomatic Service. His advent had induced the Foreign Office at once to alter the examination, and to render it, as they thought, impossible for any Titty to pass in again. The change was wise and salutary: I have sometimes felt that in occasioning this reform Titty had justified his existence. There were moments when I found it difficult to discover any other justification at all.

On that first evening, however, I found him almost impressive: there was something cosmopolitan about him; here, I felt, is a citizen of the world. I ran down the large red staircase of the Embassy and he met me on the landing half-way. He seemed very small and bony in his little dinner-jacket which displayed that right shoulder-blade, and then, a little lower down, that left shoulder-blade disproportionate to his skinny frame. From his collar emerged a peaky face, a little grey face with blue-black shadows, two small unsparkling eyes, a wet and feeble little mouth, shapeless hair. He had the sickly and unwashed appearance of an El Greco page: he perked his head on one side towards a long black cigarette-holder: his other claw-like hand clutched a grey woollen scarf: he looked infinitely childish, he looked preternaturally wizened and old. We descended to the double doorway and put on our heavy

coats and snow-boots. The air outside hit us with the
suddenness of an icy furnace, drying the galleries of
the inner nostrils like the hot-room in a Turkish
bath. We climbed into the sleigh and slid off under
the ringing night, the dry brown snow spattering
against the nets that hung behind the horses. The
padded back of the coachman loomed brown and
elephantine in front of us, but a few inches from our
knees. Titty shivered and wrapped the woollen scarf
across his nose and mouth. The ice on the Neva
where the tramway crossed it showed brown and yellow, like some ugly scab. We slid across the Troitsky
bridge and under the pencil-spire of St. Peter and
St. Paul. "What is that?" I said to Titty. He shook
his head at me, patting the woollen muffler that covered his mouth. Evidently I was not expected to talk.

[2]

The Hermitage restaurant welcomed us with a
burst of tzigane music and the smell of hot foods. In
the cloakroom were bottles of hair-wash and *violette
de parme.* Titty tried them all, he even smeared a
little solid brilliantine on his hair from an oblong
box like tooth-paste. "One's hair," he said, "gets so
scurfy with all this central heating. You should always cover your mouth when in the open air. We are
dining with d'Ormesson." He looked almost sleek as
we entered the restaurant and proceeded to the
table where d'Ormesson was reading a large menu
stamped in gold. Titty ordered some scrambled eggs,
a *gelinotte,* and a bottle of Vichy. He then gave us
back the menu and allowed us to order for ourselves.
He spoke French excellently, but not so well as I
had expected. He refused the caviare: "You never
know," he said, "where this stuff comes from." The
band at the end of the room was playing porno-
graphic music: d'Ormesson put some polite questions
to me regarding my journey. "That man over there,"

whispered Titty, "is Baron Aerenthal, the Austrian Ambassador. He's tremendously clever." "He doesn't look it," I answered, gazing at that heavy hapless face. "Well, I may be wrong," said Titty, who was always occupying positions which he at once evacuated, "perhaps he isn't clever." And at that he laughed. I felt all this, at the time, to be very diplomatic and full of meaning. It is only from subsequent knowledge of Titty that I realise that he meant nothing at all. He was singularly incapable of co-ordinating his thoughts. They were as otiose and purposeless as tourists stranded between two trains at Dortmund. They just showed themselves, walked about a bit, and went.

D'Ormesson, who was warming to the music and the red Caucasian wine, made an endeavour to render the conversation a little less desultory. He told me that he was reading Bergson and I signified polite assent. He told me that it was essential, when surrounded by the vast oppression of Russia, to have a line of conduct. I said that it must be. Above all, he felt, it was desirable to realise, while still young, one's own interpretation of the good life, one's own angle of happiness. What was mine? I was a little disconcerted by this question and mumbled something about happiness being activity in congenial surroundings. Titty turned his little face now to d'Ormesson and now to me, as if he were a seedy and embarrassed chaffinch. "Pour moi," said d'Ormesson pragmatically, "discussion d'idées générales avec des femmes supérieures." I thought this a fatuous ideal but did not say so. Titty leant forward and upset his glass of Vichy water. His little face had become taut and eager: *"I should like to be rich,"* he said. The band at this burst into a wail of Eastern-European passion: one of the white-coated violinists laid his instrument on a cane chair and proceeded to squat down and kick his legs in front of him in the Slav manner: his gipsy colleagues barked and yapped while he did it: he then regained his violin, and joined in the finale. It panted and then crashed to a conclusion. "Why do you want to be rich?" I asked Titty. "Oh, I don't know," he said, regaining his childish manner; "perhaps I don't want to be rich."

He left St. Petersburg two days later, and it was three years before I met him again. He came to see me on his way through Madrid and we dined together at the Viña P. It was I who on that occasion was obliged, alas! to drink Vichy water, but I provided for him a bottle of Pedro Jimenez. I felt that I was returning, that hot night among the fireflies, the dinner that d'Ormesson had paid for among the snow-muffled pines. He was on his way to Lisbon, he was on his way from Morocco. He had been in Madrid before, and he said "Qué tal?" to the waiters, who failed to recognise him. He told me that while at Tangier he had fallen in love with the daughter of the Portuguese Consul. "Desperately?" I inquired. "Her mother," he answered, "has got a large red birth-mark on her left cheek."

[*3*]

When I next saw him it was at Constantinople: we were colleagues there together for the two years preceding the War. I found that he had become the butt of the Chancery and that most of our spare time was to be spent in planning escapades for his entertainment. Gerald Tyrwhitt had started the pastime, and in the hands of Alec Cadogan it had been pushed to a fine art. Titty, who was senior to all of us, was head of the Chancery. He was almost incredibly incompetent, and yet he would endeavour in a forceless way to live up to his position. He told us on one occasion that it was his duty and not ours to open the red despatch-boxes that came down from the Ambassador. We took full advantage of the occasion thus afforded. We had a store in the Chancery of cardboard folders backed by a strong clamp or

spring: if one bent the folders backwards an aperture was disclosed which, when released, gripped any
papers inserted as in a vice. We discovered that if
one reversed those folders inside out and carefully
closed upon them the lid of a despatch-box, they
would, when the despatch-box was unlocked, leap
gaily three or four feet into the air. The effect was
increased if one inserted on the top little boxes of
nibs, or paper-clips, or, best of all, a tin of tooth-
powder. We would in the early morning prepare one
or two of these destructive engines, and attach a la-
bel marked "Chancery: urgent." We would then
place them among the boxes that had come down
from the Ambassador over-night. When Titty, who
was invariably late, arrived in the Chancery we
would all be working hard at our respective desks.
Titty would approach the boxes with a calm, rumi-
nating manner such as he had seen adopted by other
high officials in the past. He took hours turning over
his key-ring until he found the proper key. He had
a habit of locking up all his squalid little possessions,
so that there were a great many confusing keys to
select from. The first box contained a telegram, and
he would read it through very slowly four or five
times. Then he would exclaim suddenly in a startled
voice, "I say, you fellows, here is a telegram to go
off," and he would then place the telegram under
some newspapers, or lock it up again in the box he
had just opened, or devise some other original means
by which it might be mislaid. The second box, we
knew, was the one to startle him. Our suspense was
increased by the fact that it was again necessary for
him to search laboriously through his bunch of keys.
But when at last the key was inserted and turned, our
mechanics seldom failed to have their effect. The
folders would spring into the air with immense vital-
ity, scattering nibs and paper-clips like a handful of
flung gravel. "Oh, I say!" Titty would exclaim, "you
fellows must have been playing a joke on me." And
then very slowly, swinging his keys on a steel chain,

he would absently leave the room. The full joy of this entertainment was to be found, however, not so much in his reception of one of our explosive boxes, as in his attitude towards a box which was, in fact, authentic. He would circle doubtingly around it, fiddling with his keys, and then keep his hand very firmly down on the lid when he had at last unlocked it. Very gingerly he would relax the pressure and then, on finding that the contents were of a static and not of a dynamic nature, he would open the lid in a detached and offhand manner, as if he had known from the first that there was merely a sheet of folded foolscap inside. Alternately, when he was feeling a little below the mark, he would avoid the boxes altogether, leaving them to languish unopened for hours on end; so that in the interests of the public service this particular pastime had to be discontinued.

It was followed by others, the success of which produced a reaction. Gerry Wellesley, who is fond of children, said that really he thought we were going a little too far. Charles Lister, who possessed a heart of gold, suggested that we might leave the little fellow alone. Cadogan and I were disconcerted by this accusation of bullying, and from that moment Titty was no longer teased. He was acutely pained by this neglect. He mooned about like a lost terrier. And finally he asked me whether he had done anything to offend. Rather spiritlessly I arranged a box for him next morning. He cheered up at this and was quite happy for a week or two. But then the cholera epidemic arrived, and on its heels the first Balkan War. For the period that he remained at Constantinople Titty lived under a cloud of constant fear.

[4]

I feel that M. Euripides Stavridis, his teacher of Turkish, was to a large extent responsible for the panics which, at stated intervals, would bring Titty causelessly into my room, would lead him to pace up and down, saying that he didn't know what was the matter with him, but that somehow he felt very unwell indeed. "You should go and lie down," I said. "Oh no," Titty answered hurriedly, "you know it's a very funny thing, but it's much worse if one lies down." "You should go for a ride," I suggested. "What, out there?" Titty inquired, waving a nervous claw towards the Balkan Peninsula. "We can go to the Sweet Waters. I shall come with you." And then two days later it would all begin again. M. Euripides Stavridis was not, it must be admitted, a courageous man. He was employed during the mornings as translator at the Sublime Porte, and he would thus reach the Embassy primed with the latest news. It was a steep climb up several flights of dark stone staircase before one reached the floor allotted to the Secretaries. M. Stavridis, excessively out of breath, would sink into an armchair, place his fez on a table, mop his brow, and pant, "Deshetlü-dr, deshetlü-dr"—"It's terrible, terrible." "What's terrible?" his pupil would inquire. "Bab-alidé bir havadis var-idi che . . ." "They were saying at the Porte this morning . . ." and then would follow stories of war, pestilence and famine—not as distant or remote eventualities, but as imminent and present dangers, as something which at that very moment, among the brown roofs below us, was about to explode.

Under the cumulative effect of these unceasing menaces, Titty's brain, not in the most sedative circumstances a very taut or muscular instrument, became daily looser and looser. His thoughts appeared to flicker around his cerebral hemispheres without either direction or mutual relationship. He lost the faculty of comparison, his associations became completely haphazard, his mental exchange-system ceased almost entirely to work. I had dragged him one sullen December afternoon across the Golden

Horn and down to the sad and wintry fringe of the
Marmora. We visited St. Sergius and St. Bacchus: a
cloud of pigeons rose before us as we entered the
courtyard. "Now isn't that odd?" exclaimed Titty;
"I never knew before that Moslems believed in the
Holy Ghost." I agreed that it was odd indeed.

A few days later I was riding back after sunset,
and on passing down the Grande Rue de Péra I observed Titty in his little brown hat strolling slowly
along the pavement accompanied by two elderly men
in pearl-grey suits and yellow button boots. Titty
had many curious friends and would walk up and
down with them after tea, gazing into the wide
lighted windows of Tokatlian's Restaurant, admiring the powdered ladies who sat there drinking iced
coffee and eating little sugared cakes. This Latin
propensity of his was irritating to us, and he knew
that these his habits were disapproved. I therefore
indicated to him that evening that once again, under the street lamps of the Grande Rue de Péra, he
had been observed. "Who," I said, "were those two
men you were walking with this evening?" "Oh, *one*
of them," Titty answered, "was an Armenian." "And
the other?" I questioned. "Oh, the other," he replied
lightly, "was an Armenian too."

Such mental dislocation seriously impeded the la-
bours of the Chancery. Titty would wander nervously about the room, carrying with him the second
page of a despatch that had just been typed; he
would mislay this somewhere and spend the rest of
the morning trying to recover it: "Now that's really
very odd," he would chatter to himself, "I would
have sworn that I had the thing in my hand only a
minute ago." And thus on the days the bag went
Titty had to be locked upstairs in his room. It was
this that led him to complain to Lord Bognor.

[5]

John Everard Dunkley, third Baron Bognor, was Counsellor of the Embassy, and a man of polish and attainments. Winchester had taught him the value of mental and moral balance, and he retained for the school a deep and recurrent affection: at New College, where he rowed in the eight, he had abandoned classics and taken up history; he had an excellent memory and he obtained a very good second. He then proceeded to Potsdam to learn German and to Versailles to learn French. He was now the perfected model of a British diplomatist. His suits, which came from Sholte, were black and manly: his shirts, which came from Hopkinson, had little violet stripes and stiff collars to match: his handkerchiefs and ties, which came from Harborough's, were respectively of white cambric and grey silk: he wore no jewellery: he purchased his hairwash at the Army and Navy Stores. Twenty years of public service had slightly grizzled the fair hair which, rather long for a Wykhamist, was brushed neatly backwards above his ears: he had fine teeth, and thus a frequent and a pleasant smile: he wore an I Zingari ribbon on his straw hat, and in winter either a grey Homburg or a bowler from Lincoln and Bennett. He knew the best people in every capital in Europe and South America: he possessed even certain old and well-chosen friends among the British aristocracy. When he went home on leave he would visit his mother for three weeks at Godalming, and he would then proceed with gun and rod to Abernethy, or Gordon Castle, or a place on Deeside which had been rented by Mrs. Wickham Schultz. He possessed two top-hats and an array of boots and shoes. He was regarded by the Foreign Office not only as a sound, but also as a coming man.

Titty complained to him that I had, actually on

the morning of bag day, locked his bedroom door on the outside and taken away the key. I was sent for by Lord Bognor. I found him sitting at a large desk covered with expensive photographs in fine silver frames. His smile was infinitely agreeable, he offered me a cigarette; his method of approach was that of man, I felt, to man. "I want," he said, "to get this business cut and dried." It was irksome for me to assist him in this process of desiccation. I felt that Bognor did not care for Titty, resenting that a man of good family and public-school education should diverge so markedly from the norm. My eyes wandered idly over the photographs: "Hélène" had written the Grand Duchess Hélène: "Olga" had written the Grand Duchess Olga; and M. Béguin de Billecocq, the French Consul at Scutari, had written "Billecocq" *tout court.* "Oh," I said finally, "it was only a rag." "I see," smiled Bognor, sympathetic and broad-minded. "You must," he added with an Anglo-English wink, "consider yourself officially reprimanded." And then, with a gay note of *camaraderie* —"and what about a little bridge this evening? Oh, I forgot, you don't play. But come and dine anyhow and I'll get some kindred souls." I answered that I was engaged.

In the corridor downstairs I met Titty talking to a buck nigger. He was bowing to the man and saying, "Parfaitement, Monseigneur." I was alarmed at this, and on reaching the Chancery I inquired anxiously who it was that Titty had got hold of. They didn't know, but on Titty's table I observed a visiting card: "Moubarak," I read, "Prince héritier de Sénégambie." At that moment a clamour arose from the passage. I ran out and found the porter and two cavasses propelling the nigger towards the gateway.

"Moi," he was shouting, "Prince français!" Titty twittered nervously behind. I went up to him. "That man," he panted in great agitation, "wanted to borrow money. I don't believe he's a royalty at all. He's black." I steered Titty back to the Chancery, and he sat down staring in indignation at the visiting card before him. Suddenly he got up. "I am going to curse Marco for letting that fellow in." Marco was the porter. He resented being cursed by Titty. He appeared in the Chancery at Titty's heels. "Monsieur," he said to us, pointing at Titty with infinite scorn, "m'accuse de me mêler de la politique." Titty pretended to be suddenly busy and we smoothed Marco down. When he had gone, Titty got up and walked to the doorway. "I think," he said, "that I shall go and lie down."

[6]

Three days later we woke to hear our windows rattling to the sound of the Bulgarian guns. I had finished my breakfast and went to Titty's room. I found him sitting in a flat tin bath looking like a photograph in some pamphlet on the Indian famine. His back was turned from me, and on coming closer I was horrified to find that he was bathing in blood. "Good God, Titty, what have you done to yourself?" He turned his wizened little face towards me, and I then noticed that his eyes were full of tears. "It's permanganate," he sobbed, "of potash. One can't take too many precautions. And now they're here." "What's here?" I asked him. "Why, the Bulgars. I always told you they'd come. They are closing the shops in Galata. I heard the shutters clang as they closed them. There is certain to be a massacre. My servant has left me. All the Armenians are taking refuge on the Austrian Lloyd." I told him to dry himself and put on his clothes: he stood up while the disinfectant trickled in amethyst dribbles down his hairy little frame. I felt infinitely noble and courageous. If he had been dressed, I should at that moment have laid a firm protecting hand upon his shoulder. As it was I merely told him not to worry: that the Bulgars were twelve miles away; and that we had sent for men-of-war. He dressed nervously, but did not forget to take his medicine. He then washed his eyes in an eye-bath. He was silent and wretched. I told him that I also was terrified of cholera.

The events which thereafter followed are recounted with great realism and emotion in my novel entitled *Sweet Waters* (Constable & Co.). My friends, I find, do not rate that slim and vivid little volume at its true value. Reggie Cooper said he would not have believed it of me: Gerald Villiers said, "Mais tu en as, du toupet": Gerry Wellesley said that *he* wouldn't have dared. My intellectual friends do not mention the incident: they have read the book, since they have read every book: but they do not refer to it; they spare my feelings. Rebecca West alone showed any interest in the subject: she reviewed *Sweet Waters,* and after saying that it was silly but painstaking, expressed the conviction that my aim had merely been "to take a complex out for a run." I thought that a funny remark and of a perspicacity which seriously alarmed me. Was it true? I think it was true. I think the complex, if there was one, was repressed fear of cholera. And if that be so it had a nice little run for Messrs. Constable's money. But what right in such circumstances have I to make sport of Titty's unrepressed terror? I have no such right. The thing brooded in the battered air and crept insidiously among the dripping mud-splashed hovels of the town. I was constanly afraid. And Titty, for his part, received a telegram to say that his mother was to have a serious operation. He climbed, perky again, and with a return of his old childish giggling gaiety, on to the deck of the Rumanian steamer. He gave me some vermouth in the smoking-room: the close of Titty's adventures was thus reserved for other latitudes: he watched the Seraglio Point slip back behind Rumeli Hissar, conscious that from Constantinople at least he had escaped alive.

[7]

I am aware that at this stage, should I so desire, I could give to Titty an important or dramatic ending. After all, the European War came along, and Titty might well have been at Brussels or in the *Lusitania*. I considered this, walking up and down with Gladwyn Jebb under the plane-trees at Gulahek. But the whole point of Titty was that he existed, and that the circumstances above described were actual circumstances. My story might be a dull one, but Titty must be allowed, as God allowed him, to peter out. The owls, that moon-soaked night, answered each other from tree to tree: the crickets shrieked an undertone, continuous, bleaching, as if an emanation of the dry and crackling sun of noon. Between the trees the mountains glimmered as if lit by the headlights of some vast motor. A pond, under the oleanders, gurgled sullenly. "Yes, you are right," I said, "I must tell the truth. It is not interesting, and Titty would not have liked it. I was fond of Titty, in an unrealised way: he was one of those who taught me to break with the conventions. He was the first, I think, to show me that our inherited standards were unintelligent. He violated those standards. And yet there was something about him, there was something personal about him. I wish I knew."

"He was a friendly little man, it seems."

"Yes, I've been through that. He appeared to be. I imagined in my coarse assurance that he liked being teased. But Pierre de Lacretelle told me one evening at Therapia he had confessed that had he possessed the courage, he would gladly have poisoned either Alec Cadogan or myself."

"That was probably a moment of irritation, unco-ordinated like the rest."

"Perhaps. And yet had Titty been really tremendously rich and powerful, had it been vouchsafed to

Titty to dominate and rule, would he have been a muddled philanthropist or a bully, Semitic in his virulence and amassed self-pity?"

The owls hooted backwards and forwards, now from that tree and now from that other tree. The moon upon the pathways made wide pools of heated light. The crickets shrilled insistently, and as the moon reached them in the lily ponds, the frogs ceased to croak in lazy lechery. We turned towards the house. A lamp glimmered in my sitting-room.

"Of course, you must discount the pleasure that his insufficiency gave you: the extent to which your conceit was flattered by being able to dominate and cajole someone whom you felt you could at once patronise and ignore."

"Yes, that accounts for eighty per cent. It is the remaining twenty per cent. that puzzles me. I wish I knew."

"Well, just finish the story. You can leave the twenty per cent. I think implicit."

"I think," I said, "I shall put it down now, while I remember."

And yet what do I remember? His mother died; and Titty, only slightly enriched, was transferred to the Legation at Berne. I received a letter from him, in his strange writing, childish, undeveloped and yet surprisingly firm. He said that he liked Berne and that M. Argiatanou—did I remember that funny fellow at the Rumanian Legation?—had met him in the street. I remembered M. Argiatanou, but only as a depressing and unshaven solitary who played Bach. Titty was always unjustifiably excited by such inevitable meetings. And then, one summer, for some inscrutable reason I went with Atalanta to Interlaken. One afternoon we took tickets for an open-air performance of *Wilhelm Tell*. It is not a play that I care for, resenting the confusion between epic and pastoral. But there we were, watching the Swiss ladies sweating through their stays. And there I saw Titty sitting very good and quiet by himself in one

of the cheaper seats. I waylaid him at the entrance
and introduced him to Atalanta. She said: "You
know, there's something odd about that odd little
man. He is like Pope without the genius."

We lunched with Titty two days afterwards at the
hotel. He told us that he had spent his leave at Wies-
baden doing a cure. "It's a delightful place, Wies-
baden, it's so near Frankfurt." Atalanta, who was
not used to Titty, did not quite follow this allusion.
She looked puzzled. "Frankfurt-on-Main of course,"
Titty assured her. He had come on to Interlaken to
recuperate. His table, near the door, was covered
with medicine bottles. He cursed the waiters. It was
rather cold in the doorway and Titty explained. "I
chose the table here," he said, "because, although
there is a draught, yet I can see the people coming in
and out." "You must be rather lonely here," said
Atalanta. Titty thought that a very funny remark
and laughed inordinately. A few months later he was
transferred to Buenos Aires.

[8]

During the whole later part of the War he remained in South America, passing from place to
place. At one awful moment, owing to the death of
the Minister, he was left in charge. It took at least
three weeks before someone could be hurried there
to take his place. In the interval he sent a long and
expensive telegram to the Foreign Office which, had
it been taken seriously, would have involved us in
war with the Republic of Columbia. It was not taken
seriously, least of all by Titty himself. On the next
day he sent an even longer and more expensive telegram, saying that "on mature consideration" he had
made a mistake. He was told to shut up and to send
no more telegrams. For the rest of the War Titty remained a silent little name upon a list. In the spring
of 1920 he came home on leave. He was then down

for promotion to the rank of Counsellor, but the Foreign Office, most long-suffering of institutions, had had enough. Titty was to be offered the alternative between resignation and a very subordinate post at Adis Ababa. He came to see me in my room at the Foreign Office; he was on his way upstairs to interview the Private Secretary: I knew what they were going to say to him, but I retained a discreet and ominous silence. Titty was a little alarmed: he kept glancing at the watch which was strapped to his hairy little wrist: at two minutes to 12.0 he jumped up brightly. "Good luck!" I said to him. He promised to look in afterwards and tell me the result.

At 12.15 a delighted Titty opened the door and sat down on the edge of my table. "I must first light a cigarette," he said, and the long black holder was produced. "You know," he began at last, "such a tremendous bit of luck; they have offered me a job at Adis Ababa under Bognor. I am to start at once." "So you accepted?" "Well, of course I accepted. I have always wanted to go to Abyssinia, and Bognor is such an awfully nice chap." I looked at Titty curiously; I really think that he was being sincere. "Of course," I said, "you miss your promotion." "Oh yes, but, you see, that doesn't matter much. What matters is one's paragraph in the Foreign Office list. I know that I'm not thought very dashing or brilliant: I mistrust brilliance myself. But I swear that my paragraph in the Foreign Office list is longer than any other paragraph of my seniority." I did not pursue the subject, but when Titty had gone I pulled the Foreign Office list towards me. He was quite right. It read like a time-table. "Appointed to Lisbon June 22, 1904. Transferred to Madrid April 6, 1905. Transferred to Vienna September 1905. Transferred to Belgrade March 1906; and to Sofia August 1907; and to St. Petersburg (now Petrograd) May 1908; and to Tangier December 1908 . . ." And so on through all the capitals of Europe and South America. It was a shameful little catalogue; it spoke of a

series of intolerant chiefs stung successively to revolt. And yet Titty took a pride in his paragraph.
That was why he had welcomed Adis Ababa: it was
one of the longest names of all: would he, I wondered, have resigned if they had offered him Berne?
But I think that Titty, whatever the pressure, was
determined never to resign.

It took several weeks for him to reach Abyssinia,
and it was a month or two before Bognor's letters of
protest began to arrive. They increased in volume
and intensity. The Private Secretaries remained ob-
durate. And then one morning there came two telegrams from Bognor. Titty had caught influenza and
was seriously ill. Titty a few hours later was dead.
The will that he left behind him was so inaccurate
and confused that it entailed protracted litigation.

[9]

A year later I lunched next to Bognor at the Marlborough Club. I asked him about Titty. He adopted
the "poor little fellow" attitude, and assumed a restrained and Anglican manner when telling the circumstances of his death. "I think," he concluded, "it
was a mercy in disguise. The little blighter, you
know . . ." I was angry at this. I had since the Constantinople days increased in self-confidence. There
was now no reason why I should be polite to Bognor. I was not polite. "Why," I asked, my colour rising, "do you call him a little blighter?" "Oh well,"
he hesitated in surprise, "really, you know, between
you and me and the doorpost he wasn't quite . . ."
I looked round that ugly dining-room; at the Land-
seer prints presented by King Edward; at those
courtly servants; at those courtly old gentlemen with
their clean linen and their pearl tie-pins: I turned to
Bognor. "It is people like you," I said in a loud and
angry voice, hoping to reach the ears of the eminent
courtier opposite, of the distinguished Civil Servant

beyond, "who make diplomacy ridiculous: you sim- 'ply aren't real at all: you have got no reality: you're merely bland: that's what you are, and you're smug, you're bloody smug: absolutely bloody."

Bognor looked at me in astonishment. "You see," I added, "compared to you, Titty was a real person. You must *feel* that?" I asked him earnestly, "surely you *feel* somewhere that Titty was more of a personality than yourself?"

He changed the subject. "I see," he remarked blandly, "that George Clerk is going to Prague."

PROFESSOR MALONE

[*1*]

Eugen Malone was the old-fashioned type of journalist—the type of Vambéry, of de Blowitz, of Sir
Donald Mackenzie Wallace. The headings to his articles, which were rare and authoritative, appeared
in leaded type: he was not sent out by his paper to
the scenes of crisis, he happened invariably to be
there before, or at any rate very shortly after, the
crisis occurred: he was not a correspondent, he was
not even a special correspondent, he was just Professor Malone: and at his name the Chancelleries of
Europe used, so it was said, to tremble. In appearance he resembled Edward Fitzgerald. He was large
and lanky and had sunken eyes which he had trained
to burn with a slumbering fire; above his bushy eyebrows soared a fine forehead sweeping bonily upwards to a mane of straight grey-black hair. He did
not wear glasses, but he wore a stiff shirt and a stiff
turn-down collar, the apex of which encased a blob
of made-up tie. The cuffs above his bony wrists were
clamped by large jet links. His socks were brown and

wrinkled. Were it not for the thin edging of braid that ran along his coat, one might have taken him for a Methodist preacher: his boots in particular;— and yet there was the clip of a gold fountain pen clasping the edge of his outer pocket. His voice was reedy and gentle: he seldom spoke, but when he did speak it was with a touch of finality, with a vocal gesture as if, very softly, he were producing the ace of trumps.

I have met other publicists in my life: I have met Mr. Harold Cox and Mr. Garvin, and Pertinax and Professor Toynbee. But I have never met a publicist so supremely assured as Eugen Malone. His scholarship was incontestable; his knowledge of foreign politics sincere and unequalled: he was intimate with everybody of even incidental importance from Archangel to Algeciras; and he was always right. His gift of prophecy was in truth amazing. One would have read that morning of a massacre at Kustendil. "Ah, yes," the Professor would sigh, "it is a pity. Although I warned Guéchoff so long ago as '98. I told him at the time to keep his eye on Kustendil. But Guéchoff, as you know . . ." And at that the Professor would sigh deeply at the ὕβρις of foreign statesmen who neglected his advice. On another occasion there had been trouble in the Mirdita. The Professor smiled cadaverously: "It seems but the other day that I was last at Yildiz, yet it must be at least six years ago. Upon the wall hung a large map of what was still the Ottoman Empire. I paused before this map as I was taking leave of Abdul Hamid. I placed my finger on the Mirdita country. '*Here!*' I said. You know that way Abdul Hamid had when he was nervous? He would fiddle with the arms of his chair. 'When?' his Majesty asked me. 'In 1911, I should say.' On reaching the doorway I turned and bowed. 'Or perhaps in 1912—not later than the autumn of 1912.' I think he understood."

It is not to be supposed from such flashes of prevision that Eugen Malone was merely a speculative publicist. He knew his facts. His particular speciality was Italy. As a young man he had been intimate with Crispi and for several years of middle life had held the chair of Slav literature at Bologna University. From there his interests and his scholarship had spread in ever-widening circles. He knew all about the Ladins and the Seklers, and the Lusatian Slavs, and the Gheg colonies in Attica, and the Baranya and the Kutzo-Vlachs. He had assisted Professor Çviic in his work upon Macedonian ethnography, and had in fact prepared an English translation of that misleading volume. His rooms in South Eaton Place were stacked with brochures about the Dobrudja and the Eger enclave. He spoke a number of foreign languages with fluency and a lilting Slav accent. Nor were his attainments or his interests merely those of the scholar or the historian. He was capable of bursts of high emotion, of inspired wrath, of trenchant irony. I have heard him say some very bitter things of fallen statesmen, of Count Witte and of M. Combes. But in general he cultivated sympathy rather than abuse. "One must make allowances," he would say. "Of course I warned Bülow, and I cannot fully comprehend his present motives. But I have rather lost touch with him during the last five weeks. I should hesitate to say . . ." And of the Foreign Office he spoke with saddened sympathy, with a note of disappointed motherhood;—as if Pasteur defending the shortcomings of the Société de Viticulture at Nîmes.

[2]

As a boy I regarded Eugen Malone with unrestrained admiration. He appeared to me better than anything in Henry Seton Merriman, far, far better than anything in Mr. Le Queux. My father, who was not given to facile enthusiasms, treated the Professor with attention, almost with respect. He would say, "Well, Professor, you'll stay to luncheon; and what's the news?" The Professor would sink lankily into a leather armchair, and allow his eyes, his blazing eyes, to rest for some minutes on the portraits of former Ambassadors which adorned the walls. I offered him a cigarette—"Thank you, my boy, thank you"—and a slow meditative spiral of blue smoke would creep up against the scarlet background. "My dear Ambassador," he would begin in his gently fluting voice, "I have no news at all: it is you who have the news. I have scarcely seen anyone during the last two days beyond Stolypine and Iswolsky. Ah, yes! and Miliukoff came to breakfast with me this morning. He tells me that the Octobrists . . ." And then would follow some really startling revelation. My father sat there, picking at his thumb-nail, watching with his gay blue eyes. And after luncheon when it was all over he would say, "He's a nice old thing, Malone: so very civil."

I was therefore pleased when four years later I heard that Professor Malone had arrived at Constantinople. I asked him to luncheon in the Secretaries' mess. We were out at Therapia at the time, and we lunched under a large magnolia in the garden. I invited Lord Bognor to meet him, and the Military Attaché. He arrived late, mopping his forehead with a large white handkerchief. I introduced him to my colleagues: he treated them with gentle but rather impersonal kindness; his manner was that of the Bishop of London being presented to intending candidates for confirmation. "And how's your dear mother?" he said to Gerry Wellesley; "I hope," he said to Charles Lister, "that your dear father is well": he fixed Bognor as the one to whom, during the course of luncheon, he would address his remarks: he ignored the Military Attaché: to Titty and myself, now I come to think of it, he said nothing at all. We sat down to luncheon. Bognor, to the white sparkle of his own teeth, led the conversation. "Now

tell me, Professor . . ." The Bosphorus lapped gently against the wall outside: from time to time the
hoot of a steamer would reach us: the feet of the
servants crunched upon the gravel path: a soldier
on the wooded cliff above us was trilling a little
Turkish song. "Now tell me, Professor . . ."

I think that Eugen Malone enjoyed his luncheon.
There was, of course, that awkward moment when
Charles Lister asked him about the Turanian movement. It was not a very fair question at the date,
when Turanianism was merely a specialist theory
among the crypto-Jews. But Charles was of so modest and confiding a nature that he always imagined
that what was knowledge to him must be knowledge
to everyone. The Professor, I could see, was clearly
out of his depth. "Uranian?" he inquired, rather startled. "No, Turanian, you know—Yeni-turan." "Oh,
that," said the Professor, "that, my dear boy, is of
no importance." "But it *is,*" said Charles, putting
his head on one side and gazing at the Professor
through half-closed eyes. Bognor came to the rescue:
"I think," he said, "that what Lister means is that
the later developments of the Pan-Turk movement
are drawing the committee further and further away
from Pan-Islamism." The Professor felt ground below him: he paused; and then he slid gently into top
gear, fluting off into a very learned disquisition on
the Khalifat. Titty put on an expression as if he
knew more about it, but wouldn't say: Charles Lister continued to regard the Professor through half-
closed eyes: Gerry Wellesley confined himself to ap-
pearing discreet: the Military Attaché was slowly
scooping a melon: and Bognor nodded affably,
rhythmically, intelligently as the orator made his
points.

When it was all over there was a silence. Malone
was still slightly uneasy about Charles Lister, and
turned to me. "And how," he said, "is dear Lady
Dufferin?" I was irritated by this irrelevant inquiry

and showed it. I replied that I had no idea at all. At which there was another silence, and the Professor played his trump card.

"It is sad," he said, "about Mahmoud Shevket."

The Military Attaché dropped his melon and looked up suddenly. The smile on Bognor's face became suddenly fixed. Titty leant forward all agog— "You mean the Grand Vizier—I mean the Minister of War?"

"You have heard, of course, that he was murdered this morning at 11.15 in the Seraskerat."

"You don't say so!" exclaimed Titty nervously. Charles Lister tilted back his chair and said "Christ!" The Military Attaché banged his fist on the table. "The swine!" he said—"the bloody swine!" The perfect diplomatist, however, shows no surprise. Gerry Wellesley and I remained silent; not a muscle on our firm impassive faces stirred. Lord Bognor pulled out his handkerchief. A faint, a very faint smell of lavender-water hung for a moment in the air. "Oh dear," he remarked, and then again, "Oh dear!"

But the Professor, there was no doubt about it, had scored. It was from that moment that I began to dislike him.

[3]

The dislike which Eugen Malone had engendered that hot afternoon at Therapia simmered gently in my soul during the years that followed. It was raised to boiling-point one Saturday night in the early spring of 1917. I was at that date passing rapidly but brilliantly through my social period, and had been invited to spend Saturday to Monday with Lady Durie at Kingston. The incident which followed between myself and Professor Malone was not in itself very aggravating, but my nerves at that moment were ill-attuned. On the preceding Thursday I had dined with Archie Kerr, and he had told me some home truths. He had told me that I "failed to make myself felt." I asked him what he meant. He said that he had observed me that morning at luncheon. I had looked awkward: I had taken no part in the conversation: I had been ignored. I was annoyed at this —feeling that, on the contrary, I had had a marked, though modest, success. Sir Sidney Poole had asked me to dinner: Mrs. Lintot had called me by my Christian name: and the Grand Duke Boris had said, quite distinctly: "Monsieur, j'ai connu votre père." I told Archie that he was talking nonsense: I might be shy, but I was certainly not awkward; anyhow, we couldn't all be the play-boys of the Western world. He said that it wasn't that: it was that I was not socially authoritative: one should impose one's personality: I didn't. I must remember that I was no longer very young.

I made light of all this at the moment, but subsequently it rankled. I thought about it a good deal on the way to Coombe.

Lady Durie had bought a Tang horse. It was a nice Tang horse with chubby feet, and they were all admiring it. Eugen Malone drew me aside: "Could you tell me," he said, "who is to succeed Benckendorff?" I hesitated a moment, but Malone was not an ordinary journalist, and he had never asked me a question before. I whispered to him that they had decided to send Baron Meyendorff. "I thought," he said, "it would be Briantchaninoff." "You thought wrong," I answered sharply, remembering Archie Kerr. The Professor looked slightly taken aback at this. "Well, well . . ." he murmured. Evidently Meyendorff, at a pinch, would do. Then they all went into the dining-room. The Professor and I followed behind.

M. Cambon sat on Lady Durie's right, on her left was Mr. Winston Churchill. The other guests were only slightly less interesting and distinguished. I sat somewhere about the middle, next to Sir Seymour Fortescue: opposite to me, between the carnations,

glimmered the brow of Eugen Malone. Lady Durie
was talking about "ce pauvre cher Tsar": M. Cambon was saying "évidemment" with exquisite polish.
"And by the way," exclaimed Lady Durie generally,
"who on earth will they send to replace Benckendorff?" There was no response. I thought of Archie
Kerr, but no! With Mr. Churchill there it just
wouldn't be safe. Mr. Churchill, I have observed, has
a sharp eye for indiscretions. "Vous devriez savoir,"
said Lady Durie, leaning towards M. Cambon.
"Madame," he replied, "je suis l'ignorance même."
"Well, Winston, who is it to be?" "Don't care," mumbled Mr. Churchill. Suddenly Lady Durie's eye shot
out at me through the carnations. "Surely," she said,
"they must know by now at the Foreign Office?" "I
—I don't think it's quite settled yet," I stammered,
feeling uneasy. "Well, Professor, you who know
everything, who is it to be?" The Professor fixed me
for a moment with his slumbering eye. Everybody
stopped talking. "I understand," he said, "that the
Provisional Government have asked for the *agré-
ment* of Baron Meyendorff." "Oh, but, I say . . ."
I protested. My explosion petered out in a hum of general interest. The Professor wore upon his face the
vestige of a triumphant smile. It was then that I decided on revenge.

[4]

I had three revenges. The first was about his fountain pen: the second in connection with Essad Pasha:
the third happened two years later, and was the
more subtly satisfying of the three. The fountain pen
revenge came next day before luncheon. Malone had
given Lady Durie a copy of his book about the
Strumnitsa enclave. "Now, now, Professor, you must
write something very nice inside." In other circumstances I should at this stage have felt sorry for

Eugen Malone, knowing how awkward that business is about the something very nice inside. As things were, I was cheered by his embarrassment at finding an epigraph whereby Lady Durie and the Strumnitsa enclave could be joined upon the fly-leaf. Malone very slowly unscrewed the cap of his gold fountain pen. "What a lovely pen!" said Lady Durie.

I had seen that pen before and in a flash it all came back to me. M. Venizelos had just such another pen and so had M. Také Jonescu. I had commented on its beauty once to M. Venizelos. He had laughed and pushed his skull-cap to the rakish angle which it assumed when he was amused. "Ah oui, mon cher —figurez-vous ce pauvre Malone a une petite vanité —la Vanité des Stylos. Quand j'ai signé le Traité d'Athènes il m'a donné un stylo magnifique encrusté d'or. Il me l'a repris après la signature et l'a remplacé par un autre. Traité de Londres, même procédure: Traité de Bucarest, idem. De cette façon il collectionne des plumes historiques."

"Oh, but it *is* a lovely pen!" Lady Durie repeated. Malone allowed a little silence to intervene. "This pen, my dear lady, has a certain history. With this pen was signed the Treaty of Athens, the Treaty of London and the Treaty of Bucarest. I should not be surprised if it also signed the final treaty of peace." He held it up and let them gaze upon it. "Yes," I said in a level and incisive tone. "Venizelos told me the whole story." The Professor darted a glance at me which I returned defiantly. "Oh, do tell us, Professor . . ." The Professor was ill at ease; he hesitated. "Another time, my dear lady, another time." And then very slowly and in a large pointed hand he wrote: "To Lady Durie this story of a Balkan trouble from Eugen Malone." Mr. Churchill, who had been watching the incident, was amused. "What," he asked me, "is the truth about that pen?" I told him. I was glad to notice that the Professor saw me doing so.

[5]

I am a little distressed, on looking back, to recognise the actual malevolence which I then felt towards Professor Malone. My dislike of him now seems discreditable. Not to any important degree was he a charlatan: there was an outer edge, of course, of vanity and pretension; but the inner core was perfectly serious, the essential Malone was an honourable and high-minded scholar. It was not *his* vanity which jangled my nerves, it was my own. Had the Professor adopted towards me an attitude of even slight consideration I should have overlooked his weaknesses. It was merely because he treated me as something which wasn't there, that I desired so virulently to show him up. These considerations are obvious and need not have been underlined. I reproduce them solely because I believe that it is sometimes valuable to desiccate one's vanities and pin them on a card.

Of course I behaved caddishly towards Malone. It may be thought even that in publishing this story I am adding to my fault. But here you are wrong. Malone is not an individual but a type: the incidents recorded in this story are true incidents, but they didn't happen to Malone: had he been present, he would have behaved as I have made him behave. But he was not present. The incidents occurred without him, since Malone, except potentially, does not exist.

And yet, when I recall that night at Covent Garden, it seems almost impossible for me to disbelieve in the reality of Eugen Malone. I can see him so vividly. I can see the sharp V of his black evening waistcoat and the two coral studs above. I can see the yellow neck emerging pouched and lined from his low collar, as he strained it up and outwards like a terrapin. I can hear the crack of joints as he crossed and uncrossed his bony knees, I can hear his reedy

episcopal voice: "Ah, yes, my dear lady, yes indeed."
I can smell again the hot puffs of hair-wash and jas-
mine rising from the auditorium, the cold chalky
blast from the stage. I sat at the back of the box,
tilting my chair backwards into red shadows: in the
foreground the frame of the box cut across confused
light, beyond it and in perspective the frame of the
stage soared angular and sharply illumined: in front
two heads in silhouette—the gay and youthful head
of Mrs. Lintot, the mournful head of Eugen Malone.

[6]

"Professor," she said to him suddenly. "Do you
speak Albanian?"

The Professor hedged. "An interesting language,
my dear lady. A curious linguistic problem."

"But at least you *understand* it, Professor?"

"Oh, naturally, and I can readily make myself understood."

Mrs. Lintot gave a sharp sigh of relief and turned
her attention to the *Zauberflöte*, which they were
performing with great skill and energy upon the
stage below. I myself, being unaware of music, and
being particularly disconcerted by Mozart's habit of
never letting well alone, lapsed into reverie. I was
startled by a sudden whispered question from Mrs.
Lintot: "Tell me quick, do I curtsey to Essad Pasha?" I have a fair working knowledge of Balkan
history, and in general my memory and my associations function with average speed. But I had not
been expecting this question: I could scrape up but
the foggiest ideas of what had happened to Essad
during the War: I had almost forgotten his existence: I wasn't very sure even whether on the departure of the Prince of Wied he had or had not
declared himself Mpret. I was not positive that he
might not be dead. "Why?" I asked. My inquiry, in
the circumstances, seems wholly legitimate, but Mrs.

Lintot was clearly annoyed: she made a gesture of impatience and repeated her question hurriedly to Professor Malone. I was glad to observe that he also was somewhat at a loss. "But why on earth, my dear lady . . . ?" There was a click at the door of the box and a flood of light from the ante-room. The attendant was escorting a very upright gentleman arrayed in what is best described as full evening dress. Mrs. Lintot rose quickly and went towards him. "Altesse . . ." she said. I collected my wits. "Don't curtsey," I hissed at her. She didn't. She placed Essad Pasha beside her in the front of the box. She indicated the *Zauberflöte,* which was still proceeding undeterred by the drama in our box. "C'est magique, Altesse, storia magica." The Pasha bowed again. From his breast he emitted a loud pectoral regurgitation without which no Pasha would be complete. I leant forward. "He is not a Highness," I whispered, "he's an Excellency." Mrs. Lintot turned upon her guest a smile of sprightly comradeship. "C'est magique, Excellence." He bowed again. The Professor meanwhile had withdrawn somewhat into the shadow. He was opening and shutting his mouth like a salmon on the grass. The music below us twisted itself into quick cumulative shapes which, even to me, even from Mozart, seemed surely to indicate a finale. The curtain descended lazily. The auditorium buzzed into light and movement. Mrs. Lintot rose and led us into the little ante-room beyond.

As always, on such occasions, people came in to talk to her. There was Clifford Sharp, and Sir Vincent Caillard, and Dimitri Pavlovitch, and Countess Raben, and Anthony Asquith. Mrs. Lintot introduced them all in rapid English. "Your Excellency, this is Mr. Clifford Sharp who's very clever, and Sir Vincent Caillard who's very good-looking, and the Grand Duke Dimitri who killed Rasputin (you *did* kill Rasputin—didn't you, Dimitri?), and you *must* know Pauline—and here's our own little Puffin."

Essad bowed in silent dignity. "And oh, Professor, please explain to the Pasha that Puffin is Mr. Asquith's son." Malone, who had been making for the passage, found retreat impossible. He slowly approached Essad Pasha and addressed him in demotic Greek. His Excellency displayed polite incomprehension. The Professor tried Serbo-Croat, but again Essad remained unmoved. A certain tension descended on the company. I saw my chance and took it. I went up to Essad Pasha and pointed firmly at Puffin. "Sadarazam," I said, "oghlou." The Pasha's face radiated with relief and comprehension. He bowed deeply to Puffin. He turned to me and let fly a flood of Turkish of which a word here and there was faintly familiar to me. I answered, if not accurately, at least impressively. "Evet Pashaim—" I said, "Elbetti." And sometimes "belki," and sometimes "khair." I was much relieved, however, when the lights began to lower and the *Zauberflöte* was resumed. My precarious laurels remained unwithered. I was able to ward off disclosure till the end. And the Professor meanwhile had disappeared. Certainly it had been a triumph and a revenge.

[7]

On page 119 of the Foreign Office List will be found a menacing little paragraph entitled *"Obligation of Secrecy."* It runs as follows:—"Members of the Diplomatic Service must not, without the express permission of the Secretary of State, publish observations on, or accounts of, their experiences in the countries in which they are, or have been, officially employed, nor any information obtained by them in their official capacity. The obligation of secrecy in regard to official experience and information continues equally . . ." and the paragraph thereupon proceeds to relate what happens to indiscreet diplomatists who have already retired or who have already been dismissed. The Foreign Office is an intelligent and cheery institution and one not unduly impressed by its own regulations; but there exists a limit; there is a point beyond which even the most garish of us would hesitate to proceed. I fear, therefore, that I cannot record with any historical accuracy the drama of my third revenge on Eugen Malone. The main theme of the tragedy, the conflict of wills, can be rendered truthfully: the apparatus and setting can remain unchanged. But the actual episodes will require adjustment, the exact cause of the conflict can be rendered only in a parable. . . .

There exists, not many miles from Sicily, an island of the name of Palur. This island in the year 1908 was occupied by the Uruguayan Navy, and had remained ever since under the administration of Uruguay. The inhabitants, however, are not of Uruguayan but of Abyssinian nationality: the exact ethnical proportions are as follows:—Total population 5028: Abyssinians 4203: Greeks 403: Italians 230: Uruguayans 98: Jews 60: mixed 34. It had from the first been expected that the Abyssinians would appeal to the Peace Conference and request them to return their island. This appeal arrived from Adis Ababa some time in January 1919: the Ethiopian Government, as had been foreseen, appealed to the doctrine of self-determination. The matter was considered by the Supreme Council and a difference of opinion was disclosed. President Wilson and Mr. Lloyd George contended that the figures were conclusive and that there could be no question but that the island should be restored. Baron Sonnino, on the other hand, spoke passionately of economic interests, and argued that in any case the matter was one with which neither the Supreme Council nor the Paris Conference were legitimately concerned. President Wilson contradicted this assertion and made some very tender remarks about his and their duty to humanity. M. Clemenceau then intervened and said that the subject should be adjourned. It was adjourned for three weeks. At the beginning of February it became known that the fate of Palur was again to come before the Council.

I was sitting that morning in my office at the Hotel Astoria. It was 8 A.M. and the floor was still wet from mop and pail: the rough uncarpeted boards dried slowly round their edges, beginning near the radiator and creeping gradually towards the door. Outside, a few desultory snowflakes floated round the window, and above the flats opposite the summit of the Arc de Triomphe loomed like a vast lead coffin against a leaden sky. I was alone in my office: Allen Leeper had already left for the Quai d'Orsay: the radiator sizzled gently and from time to time the lift would hum its high continuous note. A man brought me a visiting card: "Professor Eugen Malone." The Professor, as he entered, seemed flustered and out of breath. He had come straight to the Astoria from St. Lazare: his usual languid attitude had for the moment left him: he appeared worried and at a loss; he was almost brisk. "It's about Palur," he panted. "I must see the Prime Minister at once." I stretched for the telephone and asked them to give me the rue Nitot. I told Philip Kerr that Eugen Malone wished to see the Prime Minister. "Right," he answered, "he had better come to luncheon. Twelve-thirty." I told Malone. "And at what hour," he asked, "is the Council meeting?" "At half-past two." The Professor sank back in his chair relieved. "I shall now," he said, "go and have some breakfast. I shall see you again at 11.30 and explain why I have come." His confidence had returned to him. "Don't trouble yourself, my dear boy, don't trouble."

It seemed very curious to me that the Professor should have darted across to Paris on behalf of Palur. Such dramatic alarums were uncharacteristic of him. Throughout the Conference he had remained in London, forging thunder-bolts. President Wilson had committed the mistake of leaving the White House and descending into the arena: Malone possessed a finer sense of his own dignity. Malone remained in South Eaton Place. I was so puzzled that I went along the passage and told Sir Eyre Crowe. He chuckled enigmatically. "It's about Sans Souci," he said. "What's Sans Souci?" "Malone has a villa at Palur. He calls it Sans Souci." And then he chuckled again.

At half-past eleven the Professor, calm again and again patronising, came to explain his mission. "A slight matter, my dear boy, a slight matter, doubtless. But it is the small things which lead to the sorriest blunders. All this half-knowledge, if I may say so, is very dangerous. I doubt whether a single member of the Supreme Council has ever even seen Palur." He paused. I assured him that on this point at least I shared his doubts. "Ah, yes," he sighed, "inevitable, I suppose. But I felt it my duty to warn Lloyd George. It would be terrible, terrible, were he to go off the rails in such a matter. Terrible." "But what *are* the rails, Professor?" "Why, all this nonsense about the rights of the so-called Ethiopian majority—that is, if it is a majority?" "But surely, Professor, you do not question the figures?" Malone snorted. His voice rose in sorrowing indignation. "Figures? My dear boy, allow me to tell you that this is a question of flesh and blood. Does it ever occur to you people here that you are not dealing with statistics? You are dealing with men and women, and with their children who are yet unborn. Figures, indeed! Really, things here are even worse than I imagined. Far worse." He simmered down. I asked him to elaborate his contention. He declaimed with force and sentiment upon the blessings of Uruguayan rule. The Professor was evidently not one of those who believe that self-government is better than good government. He spoke of the Ethiopian population with evident dislike. "Why, if they run themselves the island will become unfit to live in." It was the only point at which in any sense he gave himself away. We parted friends. He promised to tell me before the meeting the result of his conversation with Mr. Lloyd George.

That afternoon I was gathering together my maps and papers preparatory to the meeting of the Supreme Council. Malone appeared a little flushed by luncheon, a little flushed by success. "Well, Professor?" "Splendid, my dear boy, splendid. No one could have been more charming. I am really very grateful." "So you convinced him that Uruguay should retain the island?" The Professor beamed. "He lapped it up beautifully. I can assure you, my dear boy, he lapped it up like milk." Slowly I locked the despatch-box and tucked the maps under my arm. "Well," I said, "we shall know by this evening." I had my doubts.

[*8*]

M. Clemenceau leant forward and looked at the Agenda paper on his writing desk. "Numéro cinq," he rasped, "question de Palur." He flung his pince-nez on to the blotting-paper and sank back in his chair: his elbows rested on its arms; his lavender cotton gloves were joined in front of him clasping a yellow ivory paper-cutter the exact colour of his face. He leant his head back and his large eyelids closed: the little paper-cutter turning slowly round in those blue-gloved fingers showed that he was not asleep. Behind and above him the flaming Gobelins depicted Marie de Medicis and Henri Quatre: they soared up into that high hot room: armour, blue scarves, the smoke of distant battles among pleasant fields; and there far below them huddled the black-and-white figures of the Council of Ten: an irregular semi-circle of nine black-coated gentlemen in high-backed chairs: behind them, crushed against the heavy curtains, a thin line of secretaries and experts: upon the Aubusson carpet a litter of white papers and maps.

President Wilson stretched his legs in front of him, his two black buttoned boots tapped for a moment upon the carpet: then he withdrew them under him, leant slightly forward and began to speak. It was a clear and moderate exposition of the rights of Ethiopia: it ended on a quiet note:—"to deny such rights would not be consonant with the purposes of the United States." M. Mantoux, whose pencil had been flying across his note-book, turned back two pages and began to interpret. "Ne serait pas conforme," he concluded, "aux intentions des Etats Unis." M. Clemenceau, still with closed eyes, still holding his paper-cutter, grunted out "Les Italiens!" M. Orlando made a gesture to Baron Sonnino, indicating that it was for him to speak. The pink scalp of the Italian Foreign Minister flushed a richer shade under its stubble of white hair: it was evident that he felt very deeply on the subject of Palur. He spoke with force and eloquence of the supreme right of security and good administration: he enlarged upon the development of the sponge-fisheries so necessary for the economic existence of the island: he referred to Egypt. Mr. Balfour very gently raised his eyebrows. Mr. Lloyd George whispered to him. "A hard nut," he said, "that Sonnino." The Baron was by then entering upon his final appeal: let it not be said, he urged, that the Supreme Council had lost all touch with reality: let them act, here and now, with intelligence and with decision. Let them confirm Uruguay in her possession of the island. M. Mantoux repeated his words in English. There was a slight pause. M. Clemenceau opened his eyes: "Lloyd George," he said. The Prime Minister of Great Britain was clearly out to help. He understood, he said, the point of view of all his colleagues. On the one hand, President Wilson had reminded them, with simple and convincing eloquence, of the principles at stake: on the other hand, his friend the Italian Foreign Minister had with admirable disinterestedness reminded them of the facts. He (Mr.

Lloyd George) had given much consideration to this subject: he had that morning inclined to feel that the Italian delegation were right in their contention: this seemed a case in which these ignorant Abyssinian sponge-fishers would, in fact, stand to lose and not to gain by a rigid application of the doctrine of self-determination. The Council must remember that they were the trustees of human happiness: they must administer their trust, not blindly, but with knowledge of the facts.

Mr. Lloyd George paused at this point, making it clear by a hand slightly raised that he had more to say. M. Orlando glanced at his colleague with satisfaction. President Wilson stretched out his legs. Mr. Lansing beside him started drawing another picture of a goblin on his writing-block. M. Clemenceau slowly, and with evident enjoyment, opened one eye. "Is it *possible*," I thought in dismay, "that Malone has really induced him to change his mind?"

The head of the British delegation leant forward and adopted a conversational, almost anecdotal, tone. "Yes," he said, "when I was considering the matter this morning I had practically decided to agree with my Italian colleagues. But a strange thing happened. I had lunching with me to-day one of the greatest living authorities on Mediterranean politics, a man who, curiously enough, has first-hand knowledge of Palur. I need only mention to Baron Sonnino the name of Professor Malone to convince him that my authority for what I am going to say is not negligible. Well, the Professor is far from being unaware of the difficulties to which the Italian delegates have alluded: he said indeed that it would be difficult, very difficult, for the Abyssinian majority at once to establish an orderly administration. For several years they would require outside assistance. But he told me one thing which I have no right to conceal from the Council. He told me of the religious oppression exercised by the Uruguayan administration. It appears that the Ethiopians have an

annual festival known as 'the feast of the holy
thorn.' This festival, and the procession which accompanied it, has been ruthlessly suppressed. Among
these simple folk such stamping out of their most
cherished traditions provokes resentment and suffering such as it would be unwise for us to ignore. I
have been convinced by the picture drawn for me by
Professor Malone that this tyranny cannot be permitted. I feel that this is a case in which we must
stick to our principles whatever practical difficulties
they may involve. The island must be restored to
Abyssinia."

Mr. Lloyd George ceased speaking, and M. Mantoux translated. M. Clemenceau opened both his
eyes. "Je suis d'accord," he rasped. "Et les Italiens?"
Baron Sonnino made a helpless gesture of submis-
sion. "Et les Japonais?" The Japanese delegation
confined itself to saying how right everybody was.
"Alors c'est adopté?" said M. Clemenceau in some
surprise. There was no dissent. The ivory paper-
cutter descended like an auctioneer's hammer upon
the blotting-pad. *"C'est adopté."* I sighed with relief.
The Ethiopians, in spite of Malone, would have their
Island.

[*9*]

That evening I met the Professor at dinner. He
showed no undue anxiety to learn the result. He
seemed entirely confident that his words had produced their effect. It was only after dinner that he
came slowly up to me.

"Well, it was settled, I suppose?"

"Yes, it was settled."

"There was no difficulty, I imagine?"

"The result will probably be published to-morrow."

The Professor beamed complacently. It was not
for me to disillusion him.

"Professor," I asked incidentally, "did you say anything to the P.M. about the religious oppression of the Uruguayans?"

"No—not so far as I can recollect."

"Nothing, for instance, about the festival of the holy thorn?"

"Oh yes—I did mention it. I used the incident to show how essential it was to have a firm administration."

I smiled. I felt delighted with the Prime Minister. I felt sorry for the Professor. He had talked rather big at dinner about having come over to put Lloyd George right about Palur. He would feel a fool when he read the morning's papers.

Or would he? I am not so sure. I know only that he proceeded shortly afterwards to South America, where he played a powerful part in the dispute regarding Tacna-Arica.

ARKETALL

———

[*1*]

THE train was waiting at Victoria Station and
there remained but three minutes to the time when
it was scheduled to leave. In front of the Pullman
reserved for Lord Curzon clustered the photogra-
phers, holding their hooded cameras ungainlily. The
station-master gazed towards the barrier. Already the
two typists were ensconced in the saloon: Sir William Tyrrell in the next compartment had disappeared behind a newspaper: the red despatch-boxes
were piled upon the rack, and on the linoleum of
the gangway Lord Curzon's armorial dressing-case
lay cheek by jowl with the fibre of Miss Petticue's
portmanteau. I waited with Allen Leeper on the
platform. We were joined by Mr. Emmott of Reu-
ter's. "Is the Marquis often as late as this?" he inquired. "Lord Curzon," I answered, "is never late,"
and as I said the words a slight stir was observable
at the barrier. Majestically, and as if he were carrying his own howdah, Lord Curzon proceeded up the

platform accompanied by the police, paused for a moment while the cameras clicked, smiled graciously upon the station-master, and entered the Pullman. A whistle shrieked, a flag fluttered, the crowd stood back from the train and began to wave expectantly. It was then that I first saw Arketall. He was running with haste but dignity along the platform: in his left hand he held his bowler, and in his right a green baize foot-rest. He jumped on to the step as the train was already moving. "Crakey," said Arketall, as he entered the saloon.

[2]

Leeper and I sat opposite each other, going through the telegrams which had been sent down to the station from the Foreign Office. We sat there in the green morocco chairs of the Southern Railway: the marquetry on the panels behind us squeaked softly: the metal reading-lamp chinked ever so slightly against the glass top of the table: to our right the houses of Purley, to our left the houses of Lewisham, passed rapidly below us in the autumn sunshine: someone came and told Leeper that he was wanted by Lord Curzon. I pushed the telegrams aside and leant back in my chair. Miss Petticue was reading the *Royal* magazine: Miss Bridges was reading her own passport: I had ample time to study Arketall.

He sat opposite to me at the end of the saloon. A man, I should have said, of about fifty-five; a tall man, at first impression, with a large naked face and large white bony hands. The fine Victorian modelling of his brow and chin was marred by a puffy weakness around the eyes and mouth: at certain angles the thoughtful refinement of his features suggested a drawing of Mr. Galsworthy by George Richmond: he would then shift his position, the illusion would pass, there would be a touch of red ink

around the eyelids, a touch of violet ink about the
lips: the pallor of his cheeks, the little bleached
ridges around his mouth, would lose all suggestion
of asceticism: when he leant forward in the full light
of the window he had the appearance of an aged and
dissolute proconsul. His face, if he will forgive my
saying so, seemed at such moments, self-indulgent.
"That man," I reflected, "drinks."

I was well aware of the circumstances in which at
the last moment Lord Curzon had engaged Arketall
as his valet. Three days before we were due to leave
for Lausanne, I had walked across to Carlton House
Terrace with some papers that were urgently required. The Secretary of State was undergoing one
of his recurrent attacks of phlebitis and I was taken
up to his bedroom. I gave him the papers and he began to look at them, his lips, as was his wont, moving
rapidly in a faint, but not unpleasant, whisper as he
read the documents. My eyes wandered around the
room. It was a small room with but one window
which looked over the park: there was a white
washing-stand, a servant's chest-of-drawers, and a
cheap brass bedstead: the walls were papered with
a simple pattern of sweet-pea, and there were some
photographs and a brown wooden hair-brush upon
the dressing-table: on the small mantelpiece beside
me I noticed a washing-list, a bone collar-stud, and
two pieces of string. It was like a single bedroom in
one of the Gordon Hotels: the only luxuries were
an elaborate telephone affixed to the wall beside the
bed, and a large box of crystallised fruits upon a side-
table. The problem of Lord Curzon's personality,
which had become almost an obsession to me, was
enhanced by the sight of these accessories. My eyes
wandered round the room in mute surprise. They
returned finally to the figure in the bed. He was no
longer looking at the documents, he was looking at
me. "You are observing," he said, "the simple
squalor of my bedroom. I can assure you, however,
that my wife's apartments are of the most unexam-

pled magnificence." And at this his shoulders shook
with that infectious laughter of his, that rich
eighteenth-century amusement. "You have also," he
continued, "observed the telephone. A disastrous in-
vention, my dear Nicolson, but it has its uses. Thus
if I make upon this ivory lever a slight pressure to
deflect it to the right, a mere *exiguum clinamen,* the
whole secrets of my household are revealed to me. I
overhear. This morning, for instance, when thus
switched on (I think that is the correct term) to the
universe, the bell rung. A voice said, 'Is that you,
Alf, and 'ow's it feeling this morning? I 'ad a devil
of a time coming in with the milk like that.' 'My
dear young lady,' I answered, 'you are singularly mistaken. You are not speaking to Mr. Alfred Horlick,
you are speaking to Lord Curzon himself.' The noises,
I may say, which greeted me from the other end indicated that my words had produced an effect which
was positively blasting. And Horlick, an excellent
valet, leaves me to-morrow."

Victim of such coincidences did Arketall sit there
that morning in the Pullman with a small and
incongruous bowler perched upon his head. He became slightly uneasy at my scrutiny: he reached for
his suit-case and extracted *John o' London's Weekly:*
I returned to my telegrams. The train skimmed tin-
kling and direct above the Weald of Kent.

[3]

Our arrival at Dover somewhat disconcerted Arketall. It was evident that he was proud of his compe-
tence as a travelling valet and anxious to win confidence by a brisk display of merit. Before the train
had come to a standstill he was out on the platform,
his face assuming the expression of "Leave everything to me." He was at once brushed aside by an
inspector of police and two Foreign Office messengers. A phalanx of porters stood behind the inspec-

tor and leapt upon our baggage. The Foreign Office
messengers seized the despatch-boxes. Before Arketall had realised what had happened, Lord Curzon
was walking slowly towards the boat chatting to the
inspector with not unconscious affability. We strolled
behind. Arketall came up to me and murmured
something about passports. I waved him aside. There
was a man beside the gangway with a cinematograph,
the handle of which he began to turn gently as we
approached. I glanced behind me at Arketall. His
attitude had stiffened suddenly into the processional.
"Arketall," I said to him, "you have forgotten the
foot-rest." "Crakey!" he exclaimed as he turned to
run towards the train. The other passengers were by
then beginning to dribble through the pens in which
they had been herded: I leant over the taffrail,
watching the single agitation meeting the multiple
agitation: widows hurrying along searching franti-
cally in their reticules for those yellow tickets which
would take them to Bordighera: Arketall, in acute
anxiety, breasting this fumbling torrent with his
bowler in his hand. A policeman touched me on the
shoulder: he was holding the foot-rest. "His lordship
generally requires this with him on the voyage." But
by then Arketall was but a distant dome-shaped
head bobbing against a panic stream. The little
cords that tied the awning above me were pattering
against the stays in an off-shore wind: in the gap between the pierheads a swell tumbled into foam, the
inner harbour was wrinkled with scudding frowns:
clearly we were in for a rough crossing. I took the
foot-rest to Lord Curzon. He was sitting at his cabin
table writing on loose sheets of foolscap in a huge
flowing hand: his pencil dashed over the paper with
incredible velocity: his lips moved: from time to time
he would impatiently throw a finished sheet upon the
chintz settee beside him. I adjusted the foot-rest. He
groaned slightly as he moved his leg. He was much
too occupied to notice my ministrations. I returned
to the deck outside. A voice wailed to me from the

shore: "It's gone; it's gone." Arketall flung into the
words that forlorn intensity which throbs in the earlier poems of Lord Tennyson. I replied by reassuring
gestures indicative that he should come on board. He
was mopping his forehead with a large linen handkerchief: little white drops were still forming on it
as he stood panting beside me. "Crakey!" he gasped.
"You had better go downstairs," I answered, "it is
going to be rough." He closed one eye at me. "A little peg, Ay don't think." His words, at the moment,
had little apparent meaning.

[4]

I did not see Arketall again until we were approaching Calais. I found him talking to Sir William
Tyrrell outside the cabin. "Now, Ostend," he was
saying, "that's another question. Nane francs a day
and no questions asked." "And no questions asked,"
he repeated, looking wistfully at the sand dunes.
The inspector came up to me with a packet of passports: he said he would hand them over to the *com-
missaire de police* on arrival. I took them from him,
desiring to solve a problem which had often assailed
me, namely, whether Lord Curzon made out a passport for himself. It was there all right—"We, George
Nathaniel," and then his name written again in the
blank spaces. That amused me, and I was still considering the curious associations evoked by such official Narcissism when we sidled up to the Calais
landing-stage. The gangway was immediately opposite Lord Curzon's cabin: on the pier below stood the
Consul in a top-hat, and some French officials: I went
in to Lord Curzon and told him we were arriving:
he was still writing hard, and paid no attention: on
the settee beside him was a pile of foolscap and at
least twenty envelopes stamped and addressed. A
muffled jerk showed that we were already alongside.
Sighing deeply Lord Curzon addressed and stamped

the last envelope. "Send me that valet man," he said. I fetched Arketall, telling him to hurry as the other passengers were being kept waiting: there they were on my left secured by a cord across the deck, a serried wedge of passengers looking their part. Lord Curzon emerged genially from his cabin at the exact moment the gangway was fixed: Arketall followed with the foot-rest: he stumbled as he stepped on to the gangway and clasped the rail. "Yes, I thought he was drunk," said Sir W. Tyrrell as we followed in our correct order. Lord Curzon was being greeted by the Representative of the French Republic. He moved slowly towards the train, leaning on his ebony cane; behind him zigzagged Arketall, clasping the green baize foot-rest. "Hadn't we better warn the Marquis . . . ?" I asked. "Oh, he'll notice it soon enough." Lord Curzon had paused by the train to say a few chosen words to the Consul. Behind him stood Arketall, very rigid as to the feet, but swaying slightly with the upper part of the body, bending slowly forwards and then straightening himself with a jerk. We left for Paris.

[5]

The next thirty-six hours are somewhat of a blur in my memory. I can recall M. William Martin at the Gare du Nord and other top-hats raised simultaneously, and the flash and subsequent smell of magnesium wire lighting rows of white featureless faces beyond the barrier: a group of Americans pausing to stare at us, cocktail in hand, as we entered the Ritz—"Why, look, Mrs. Cameron . . ." and then the figure of Mr. Ellis, pale and courtly, standing erect beside Lord Curzon in the lift: the corridor stretching white, airless, unwindowed, the little lighted globes in the ceiling, the four detectives grouped together, a bottle of Evian and two glasses on a Saratoga trunk. I remember also a late dinner and Olivier ministering to Lord Curzon and yet not ignoring us—Olivier blending with a masterly precision the servile and the protective, the deferential and the condescending. And then the following day the familiar conference atmosphere: the crackle of Rolls-Royces upon the raked and watered gravel in front of the Affaires Etrangères: the slow ascent, maps, despatch-boxes, politeness, up the wide stone staircase: the two *huissiers* in evening dress and silver chains, that *huissier* with a white nose, that other *huissier* whose nose is red: the first ante-room, gold and damask, the second soft-carpeted ante-room, damask and gold: the Salle de l'Horloge—green rectangles of tables, a perspective of pink rectangles of blotting-paper: M. Poincaré advancing from a group by the furthest window: the symmetry of alignment broken suddenly by papers on the green cloth, protruding edges of maps, despatch-boxes with open lids, secretaries bending from behind over their employers, the interpreter sitting with his pencils and note-book by himself: the soft hum of traffic along the Quai d'Orsay.

We lunched that day with Madame Poincaré and afterwards the discussions continued: at 4 P.M. the chandeliers leapt in successive tiers to brilliance; the white and scarlet benches in the window recesses were hidden one by one as the silk curtains were drawn across them, and at five we had tea and macaroons in the large white room beyond. At nine we returned exhausted to our dinner; we were all to start for Lausanne next morning at 7.30.

We gathered sleepily at 7.5 A.M. in the hall of the Ritz: the revolving glass door was clamped open and a man in a striped apron was shaking an india-rubber mat out on to the Place Vendôme: the luggage had already preceded us, the typists were sitting in the third motor rather pinched and blue: we waited for Lord Curzon. At 7.16 A.M. he appeared from the lift escorted by Mr. Ellis. He climbed slowly into the motor, falling back on to the cushions with a sigh of pain: he beckoned to me: "I shall want my foot-rest." I dashed back into the hotel to search for Arketall. Mr. Ellis was standing by the staircase, and as I approached him I could hear someone pattering above me down the stairs: at the last turning there was a bump and a sudden exclamation, and Arketall shot round and down the staircase like a bob-sleigh, landing beside me with his feet in the air and the foot-rest raised above him. "Crakey!" he remarked. We had by then only eleven minutes in which to reach the Gare de Lyon. The three motors swayed and dashed along the boulevards like fire-escapes to an incessant noise of Klaxons. Then very slowly, processionally, sleepily we walked up through the station towards the platform. M. Poincaré in a black silk cap with a peak was waiting, a little irritably I thought, beside the train. There was a saloon for the French delegation, a saloon for the British delegation, and separating them a satin-wood drawing-room carriage and a dining-car. The large white clocks marked 7.29 as we entered the train. At 7.30 we slid out into the grey morning past a stiff line of saluting police and railway officials. Arketall was standing beside me: "Ay left me 'at behind," he remarked in sudden dismay. I had a picture of that disgraceful bowler lying upwards on the stair carpet of the Ritz: "Tiens," they would exclaim, "le chapeau de Lord Curzon." "You can get another," I answered, "at Lausanne." Miss Petticue came up to me holding a bowler. "They threw this into our motor as we were leaving the Ritz." I handed it in silence to Arketall.

[6]

For the greater part of that twelve-hour journey we sat in the drawing-room carriage discussing with our French colleagues the procedure of the impending conference: from time to time a Frenchman would rise and retire to the back of the train to consult M. Poincaré: from time to time Allen Leeper or I would make our way to the front of the train to consult Lord Curzon: outside his door Arketall sat on a spring bracket-seat which let down on to the corridor: he would stand up when we came, and the seat would fly up smack against the wood-work: Arketall looked shaken and unwell. Lord Curzon in his *coupé* carriage reclined in a dove-coloured armchair with his leg stretched out on the foot-rest. On the table beside him were at least thirty envelopes stamped and addressed: he did not appear to relish our interruptions.

Towards evening the lights were lit in that satin-wood saloon. We sat there, M. Barrère, General Weygand, Admiral Lacaze, Sir William Tyrrell, Laroche, Massigli, Allen Leeper and myself. The discussion had by then become desultory: from time to time a station would leap up at us from the gathering dusk, flick past the train in a sudden rectangle of illuminated but unfocussed shapes, be lost again in the brooding glimmer of the Côtes d'Or. We stopped at Pontarlier and telephoned to M. Mussolini. He answered from Locarno. He wanted us to dine with him that night at Vevey. We pattered up and down the platform conveying messages from M. Poincaré to Lord Curzon, from Lord Curzon to M. Poincaré. It was agreed that they would both proceed to Vevey, and then the train slid onwards down upon Lausanne. Lord Curzon in his dove-coloured armchair was slightly petulant. He was all for dining with M. Mussolini but would have preferred another night. "And why Vevey?" he said. "Why indeed?" I echoed. Lord Curzon sighed deeply and went on writing, writing. I left him and stood in the corridor. Arketall had pulled up the blind, and as the train jigged off to the left over some points a row of distant lights swung round to us, low-lying, coruscating, white and hard. "Evian," I said to Arketall. "Ho indeed," he answered. Ten minutes later, the train came to rest in the station of Lausanne: there was a pause and silence: the arc-lamps on the platform threw white shapes across the corridor, dimming our own lights, which but a few minutes before had seemed so garish against the darkness. I returned to Lord Curzon's compartment. "I think," he said, "that you and Leeper had better get out here. It is quite unnecessary for you to come on to Vevey." "Oh, but, sir . . ." I protested. "Quite unnecessary," he repeated. I usually enjoyed an argument with Lord Curzon, but there was something in his voice which indicated that any argument at that moment would be misplaced. I went and told Leeper: we both seized our despatch-boxes and climbed down on to the platform. Bill Bentinck, who had been sent on two days before to complete arrangements, came up to us, immaculate, adolescent and so reliable. "There are four motors," he said, "and a lorry for the luggage." "The Marquis isn't coming," I informed him, "he and M. Poincaré are going on to Vevey to dine with Mussolini. They won't get back here till midnight." "Oh Lud!" he exclaimed, "and there's a vast crowd outside and the Mayor of Lausanne." "Lud!" I echoed, and at that the slim Presidential train began to slide past us towards the night and Mussolini. It was only then that I noticed that the platform was empty from excess rather than from lack of public interest: behind the barrier, behind a double row of police, stretched the expectant citizens of the Swiss Confederation. On the wide bare desert of the platform stood Leeper in a little brown hat, myself in a little black hat, and Arketall in his recovered bowler: Miss Petticue: Miss Bridges: pitilessly the glare of forty arc-lamps beat down upon our isolation and inadequacy. We walked (with dignity, I feel) towards the barrier: at our approach the magnesium wire flashed up into its own smoke and there was a stir of excitement in the crowd: somebody cheered: Arketall raised his bowler in acknowledgment: the cheers

were repeated: he held his bowler raised at exactly
the correct angle above his head: the Mayor advanced towards him. I intervened at that moment
and explained the situation. The Mayor turned from
me, a little curtly perhaps, and said something to the
police inspector. The wide lane which had been kept
open for us ceased suddenly to be a lane and became
a crowd leaving a station: we left with it. In a few
minutes we were hooting our way under the railway
bridge and down to Ouchy.

[7]

The hall of the Beau Rivage was crowded with
hotel managers and journalists. The former bowed
ingratiatingly at our entry: the latter, who had been
sitting together at little tables drinking sherry, rose
as a man to greet us. There was Mr. Walker, and
Mr. Pirrie Gordon, and Mr. Ward Price, and Mr.
Ryall. There were a great many others whom I did
not know: they looked diverse and yet convivial: I
like journalists in principle and was extremely sorry
to disappoint them: at no moment of my life have I
desired so acutely to be important. Through all this
gratuitous humiliation I was conscious, however, of a
thin thread somewhere within me of self-esteem. I
lay idly in my bath trying to work this vaguely apprehended fibre of pleasure into the central focus of
my consciousness, which seemed in its turn wholly
occupied by pain: I tested myself in successive
phases: the platform, solid pain: the exit from the
platform, pain unrelieved: it was only when I went
back to the phase in the motor that I ceased inwardly
to wince. Leeper, rather tired and thinking silently
about Rumania, had sat beside me; but Arketall,
on the *strapontin* opposite, was full of talk. "Very
civil," he had said, "these Swiss people. Now Ay remember when Ay was with a Columbian gentleman,
we went to Zurich. You know Zurich, sir? Well, it

was lake this . . ." Yes, Arketall at that moment had
called me "sir": up to that moment he had treated
me solely as a colleague. Something in the force of
my personality or in Lord Curzon's absence had ele-
vated me to a higher level of regard. I was gratified
on discovering this, and lay back in my bath thinking affectionately of Lord Curzon, who at that moment must have been descending on to the platform
at Vevey. Sir William Tyrrell would have to carry
the foot-rest: I did so hope that, if Lord Curzon got
tired, Sir William would be able to soothe him down.

We dined downstairs in the restaurant. The re-
mainder of the delegation had assembled by earlier
trains There was General Burnett-Stuart with a
military staff, and Sir Roger Keyes with naval assist-
ants: there was Mr. S. D. Waley of the Treasury,
and Mr. Payne of the Board of Trade: our own Sec-
retariat was under the charge of Tom Spring Rice:
there was a young man of extreme elegance who
looked after the maps: there was an accountant and
two further lady typists, and there was Mr. McClure
for the Press. Undoubtedly we were an imposing collection. M. Duca and M. Diamandy, the Rumanian
representatives, were seated at a further table; they
came across to us and gave us caviare out of a flat
tin box. I was pleased at this, mainly for Allen Leeper's sake, since, although in general the most stimulating of companions, he is apt at moments to brood
about Rumania in silent suffering: with their arrival
his pang had found a voice. It was a pleasant dinner if I remember rightly, and when it was over,
Leeper and I ascended to put the final touches to
Lord Curzon's suite. A large drawing-room on the
first floor gazing from its three high windows upon
the lake: on the left a dining-room, on the right a
bedroom with baths beyond. The drawing-room was
sprinkled with little white armchairs and tables looking very occasional: there were palms and chrysan-
themums in a large brass *jardinière:* there was a
little bean-shaped bureau, and on the walls some col-

oured prints of ladies in green riding-habits descending the steps of Chambord, Chenonceaux and Blois. We removed these pictures and secured a larger writing-table. We sent for more flowers, and arranged some newspapers and brandy and soda upon a side-table. In the bedroom next door Arketall was unpacking several trunks: I looked in on him: he was not inclined for conversation, but hiccoughed gently to himself as he swayed, now over the Marquis's black suits and now over his grey. It was by then 11.30: a telephone message came in from Vevey to say that Lord Curzon should reach Lausanne about midnight: we descended to the hall to await his arrival.

[*8*]

At 12.10 there was a stir at the front door and the managers dashed to the entrance. They returned in triumph, escorting a small brown gentleman in a brown suit and very white shirt-cuffs. He carried a brown bowler in his left hand and his right was thrust into his waistcoat. The iris of his eyes was entirely surrounded by white, a phenomenon which I had hitherto observed only in the photographs of distinguished mesmerists. He was followed by three or four other gentlemen and two boy-scouts in black shirts. An electric tremor ran through the assembled journalists. "Mussolini," they whispered in amazement. I turned to Allen Leeper. "Really," I remarked, "that was very odd indeed." "It was," he answered.

Ten minutes later the glass doors again gyrated and Lord Curzon, magnificent and smiling, stood upon the threshold. Slowly and benignly he bowed to the managers: to the journalists he made a friendly gesture at once welcoming and dismissive: he proceeded to the lift. Seizing the green foot-rest from Sir William Tyrrell, I hurried through the

crowd towards the staircase: "Tiens," exclaimed a
French journalist, indicating the foot-rest, "le trône
de Bagdad." I pushed past him and arrived on the
first floor just as Lord Curzon was leaving the lift.
He paused at the doorway of his apartment and
surveyed it. "How ghăstly!" he sighed. He walked
towards the window, pulled aside the yellow cretonne curtain, and gazed across to the lights of
Evian. "How positively ghăstly," he repeated. We
helped him out of his large Lovat-mixture greatcoat;
we propped the ebony cane against the white wall:
we pulled up the least diminutive of the sixteen
armchairs, and we placed the foot-rest in position.
He sank back, sipped at a brandy-and-soda, sighed
deeply, and then embarked on a narrative of the
Vevey conference.

Ah, those Curzonian dissertations! No small thing
has passed from my life now they are silenced. As if
some stately procession proceeding orderly through
Arcs de Triomphe along a straight wide avenue: out-
riders, escorts, bands; the perfection of accoutre-
ments, the precise marshalling of detail, the sense of
conscious continuity, the sense of absolute control.
The voice rising at moments in almost histrionic
scorn, or dropping at moments into a hush of sudden emotion; and then a flash of March sunshine, a
sudden dart of eighteenth-century humour, a pause
while his wide shoulders rose and fell in rich amusement. And all this under a cloud of exhaustion, under a cloud of persistent pain.

The glamour of this particular discourse was somewhat dimmed for me by anxiety on behalf of Arketall. The door into the bedroom was open, and there
came from it the sound of cupboards opening and
shutting, the sound at intervals of a hiccough inade-
quately suppressed. "We had by then," Lord Curzon
was saying, "reached the last point of the six which
I have grouped under category A. Mussolini had as
yet not fully grasped my intention; with the assistance of that dilapidated marmoset who acts as his

mentor I regained my point of departure: the status of *pertinenza,* I explained . . ."

" 'Ic" came loudly from the adjoining room. Lord Curzon paused. My eyes met those of Allen Leeper and I motioned to him to close the door.

". . . the status of *pertinenza,* I explained, was in no way identical with what we regard as domicile. Poincaré, who on all such points is exăsperatingly punctilious, insisted on interrupting. He maintained . . ."

" 'Ic," said Arketall from the next room. Leeper had by then reached the doorway and closed it abruptly. "What was that?" said Lord Curzon, turning a petulant eye in my direction. "It is your servant, sir, unpacking some clothes."

"He maintained that the *droit d'établissement* . . ." The procession had re-formed and continued its stately progress: it continued until 2 A.M.: the Marquis then dismissed us: he said he had letters to write as well as a report for the Cabinet; he had by then to our certain knowledge been working without interruption for nineteen hours; and yet in the morning there was a report of eight pages for the Cabinet, and on the table in the passage twenty-two letters addressed and stamped—or, as he himself would have said, "stamped and directed."

[9]

Next morning there was to be a meeting to continue the conversations begun at Vevey. We arranged a large table in Lord Curzon's room and placed paper and pencils at intervals. The Marquis sat at his desk writing rapidly. Punctually at eleven both doors were flung open by Arketall. "Excellence Poyncarry," he bawled, "and General Wiggand." Lord Curzon rose genially to meet them, and conducted them to the table. They sat down and waited for M. Mussolini. General Weygand began drawing little squares and triangles on the sheet before him. Poincaré rose and walked up and down the room in obvious impatience, flicking his pince-nez against his thumb-nail. From time to time he would pause at one of the windows, looking at the grey fog which crept among the conifers. Lord Curzon kept on sending me with messages to the Duce urging him to come. I did not execute these missions, knowing them to be of no avail, but I had several pleasant chats in the passage with Mario Pansa, who was acting as M. Mussolini's personal secretary. From time to time I would return to Lord Curzon's room and assure them all that M. Mussolini was on his way. I would then resume my talks with Mario, whose gay Harrovian chatter relieved a situation which but for him I might have found a trifle tense. When, at 11.35, M. Mussolini actually did come, he came very quickly. Pushing Arketall aside, His Excellency shot into the room like a brown thunderbolt, stopped short, clicked his heels, bowed and exclaimed, "Je vous salue, Messieurs." They then sat down at the table, and we sat behind. The maps were spread in convenient places; the interpreter sharpened his pencil. The Vevey conversations were resumed.

That evening M. Poincaré returned to Paris, and M. Mussolini to Rome: Lord Curzon was left pre-eminent over a conference consisting mostly of Ambassadors. There was M. Barrère and M. Bompard for France: and for Italy the aged Marchese Garroni: Ismet Pasha, deaf and boyish, coped with a large and resentful Turkish delegation: M. Venizelos, troubled but conciliatory, spoke for Greece: at moments, even, the mezzo-soprano of M. Tchicherine would quaver into our discussion. And as the days passed, Arketall, to my despair, entered visibly on a decline.

[10]

We found it difficult to induce Lord Curzon to treat the problem seriously. On the second morning Arketall, in helping his master on with his socks, had slipped and fallen. "Arketall," Lord Curzon had remonstrated, "you are either very ill or very drunk." "Both, m' Lord," Arketall had answered. Lord Curzon was so pleased with this response that his affection for Arketall became unassailable. We grew seriously uneasy. I found him one morning standing by the side-table in the dining-room pouring liqueur-brandy into a claret glass. He winked slowly at me and placed a shaky forefinger beside his nose. I was incensed at this gesture of confederacy: I told Bill Bentinck that the Marquis must again be warned. But unfortunately that morning Marchese Garroni had, in Lord Curzon's presence, mistaken Arketall for Sir Roger Keyes, had seized both his hands and had assured him in a torrent of Genoese French how great a debt, how unforgettable a debt, Italy owed to the noble and generous British Navy. Lord Curzon was so delighted by this incident that our warnings fell on even deafer ears. A catastrophe was imminent, and it came.

The Hôtel Beau Rivage at Ouchy consists of two wings joined together by a large suite of ball-rooms and dining-rooms. In the evening the natives of Lausanne and the visitors undergoing either education or treatment would gather in the foyer to listen to the band, to watch the dancing, and to observe the diplomatists and journalists passing backwards and forwards on hurried and mysterious errands. Saturday was the gala night, and on Saturdays I would generally slip down after eleven and sit there admiring the couples jerking together in the ball-room. There was an American woman of great distinction, who wore a stomacher of diamonds: there was a greedy-looking Cuban woman in a wheeled basket chair: there was Prince Nicholas of Russia, who was staying at a neighbouring *pension* and who danced with all the young ladies. It was a pleasant sight, and on the second Saturday I induced Lord Curzon to come and watch it. He stood there by the entrance to the ball-room leaning on his ebony cane, and smiling genially at the diverse couples who jigged and twirled before him. I observed the American lady syncopating towards us in the arms of a distinguished-looking gentleman in evening dress. I called Lord Curzon's attention to her, warning him to observe her stomacher as she passed. He glanced towards her and grasped my arm. "Surely," he said, "surely that can't be Arketall?" It was Arketall, and he recognised us at the same moment. In trying to wince away from the cold inquiry in Lord Curzon's eye, he slipped between the legs of the American lady and brought her down upon him. Lord Curzon had turned abruptly and was walking back across the foyer. I ran after him. "I think," he said, "that Arketall had better leave. He had better leave early to-morrow."

I returned to the ball-room and accompanied Arketall to his room. He was somewhat dazed by his experience and he followed me meekly. I told him that there was a train at 7.30 next morning and he had better leave by it. He plunged under the bed and began pulling out his portmanteau: it refused to move and he tugged at it viciously: three empty bottles of Benedictine and a bottle of Grand Marnier shot out into the room, followed by the trunk. Arketall sat on the floor, nodding at the empty bottles. "You must pull yourself together," I said. "You should at least assist us to minimise the scandal which your conduct has caused." "Never," he hiccoughed vaguely, "not no more."

[*11*]

I did not witness his departure. I merely heard next morning that he had gone. While having breakfast I received a message that Lord Curzon wished to see me urgently. I found him in his dressing-gown. He was half angry and half amused. "That indefinite Arketall," he said, "has stolen my trousers." "Not *all* your trousers?" I asked in some confusion. "Yes, *all* of them, except these." Lord Curzon was wearing his evening trousers of the night before. I glanced at my watch. There was still an hour before the meeting of the Conference, but by this time Arketall must have reached Pontarlier. I ran for Bill Bentinck and told him to telephone to the frontier police: "Don't say trousers," I shouted after him, "say 'quelques effets.'" I then secured the manager and proceeded to Arketall's room. We looked in, over and under the cupboard and into the chest of drawers: I peered under the bed; there were three more bottles of Benedictine against the wall, but otherwise the space was empty. The manager and I looked at each other in despair. "C'est inénarrable," he muttered, "complètement in-é-narrable." I sat down wearily on the bed to consider our position. I jumped up again immediately and pulled back the bed-spread. Upon the crumpled bed-clothes lay a trouser-press bursting with Lord Curzon's trousers. I sent the manager to stop Bill Bentinck telephoning; myself I clasped the trouser-press and returned in triumph to Lord Curzon. He was seated at his writing-table, his pencil dashing across sheets of foolscap, his lips moving. I stood there waiting. When he had finished four or five sheets and cast them from him he turned to me indignantly. His face relaxed into a smile and then extended into that irresistible laugh of his, that endearing boyish sense of farce. "Thank you," he said, "I shall now complete my toilet. There will only be

Leeper to dinner to-night, and as a reward I shall give you my celebrated imitation of Tennyson reciting 'Tears, idle tears.' "

He kept his promise. It was an amazing performance. We expressed our admiration and our gratitude. A sudden wave of depression descended upon Lord Curzon. "Ah, yes," he sighed, "ah, yes. I know. All that was years ago, when I was young and could still läugh at my elders. But all young men are remorseless. You will go upstairs this evening and chäff me behind my back. You will give imitations in after life of the old buffer imitating Tennyson. And so it continues." He sighed deeply. And then he grinned. "I am sorry," he said, "for Arketall. I liked that man."

MIRIAM CODD

[*1*]

"Excuse me, sir, but could you tell me the name of that island?"

I turned and looked at her.

"That, Madam, is the island of Cerigo, better known as Cythera, and famous for the cult of Aphrodite."

She received this statement with gentle indifference.

"The one beyond," I continued, "has several names. It is called Cerigotto or Anti-Cythera, or Lius: to the ancients it was known as Ægilia or Ogylos."

She gazed up at me with blue but meditative eyes.

"Excuse me, sir," she began again, "but are you any relation to Sir Ronald Storrs?"

"I am afraid not, Madam—not in any way."

She sighed at this. "You are so like him," she added.

I was not at all displeased at having evoked this association. Storrs, it is true, is a slightly older man than I, but his face at least is ardent and pro-consular. I have often envied him, as I have envied Gerry Wellesley, the faculty of giving people rapid and often accurate information. So I spoke to her politely. "I like Sir Ronald Storrs," I said, "and I have followed his career with interest and admiration. But we are not, I regret to say, related."

She sighed again and looked away from me out across the Ægean. Her eyes, which were fixed disapprovingly upon Cythera, were the colour of the intervening sea. Her little podgy hand clasping the *Saturday Evening Post* displayed a large cabuchon sapphire. It was the colour of her eyes. For the rest, she was completely round—she represented two superimposed circles like the figure eight or a very neat and new cottage loaf. She was small and mild and gentle and wrapped in a series of blue silk scarves that matched her eyes. One felt that for forty-five odd years she had eaten expensive candy, and drunk a great deal of iced water, and had at least 34,000 baths, and worn very clean and fleecy underclothing. I was somewhat desolate at the time, and the abundant maternal instinct which exuded from her as lanoline from a tube was not unpleasurable. I smiled down upon her deck-chair, hoping that she would smile up from it at me. She did nothing of the sort. She was still gazing with marked discontent at the amethyst contours of Cythera.

"And so that," said Miriam Codd, "is Cyprus."

[2]

The s.s. *Helouan* rolled slumberously in the warm November sunshine on her way to Alexandria. The rubber soles of Colonel Pomeroy went flip-flap, flip-flap on the planks as he walked eager and exultant round and round the promenade deck: every seven minutes he would pass my chair, and his exultant monologue would swell out and then decrease again:

". . . by a man called Lawrence. Upon my word there are pages in that book which ought to be taken out and burnt. Clever, I grant you, but what I always say . . ." Major Tweedie trotted acquiescent beside him. Seven minutes would elapse and then that confident gait, that exultant voice, would again intrude upon my consciousness:—"Rotten, my boy, that's what I call it, rotten. And mark you, I've known Joynson-Hicks since we were kiddies together. Not but what . . ." I lay back and watched the evening sun advance and recede across the sharp tarlines in the deck: from time to time there would be a heavier roll and the sunlight would swing up to my feet, pause a moment, and then retreat again. The shadows of the stanchions supporting the upper deck were elongated and then again foreshortened in the process. And behind it all, outside the focus of consciousness, came the swish and tumble of the sea, the sound of stewards rattling the dinner-plates in the saloon. How much I dislike the melancholy of these marine and steamship sunsets! The sunlight in its rhythmic swaying takes on a yellow, and then an orange, and then a scarlet tinge: the waves turn cold and purple: the miserable lights are lit along the deck, desolate and feckless points of security against a growing menace: the sea frowns and becomes aloof and limitless: the ship, no longer buoyant and foam-sounding, cowers inert, puny, helpless and engulfed. The spray seethes and sighs around one with the hiss of death. I rose dejectedly and went into the music-room.

There was a young Polish gentleman at the piano playing Ravel. I knew it was Ravel because, on passing behind the piano, I had seen the name written quite distinctly below the word *"Suite."* I had met M. Ravel once (a miffy little man) lunching with Lady Colefax; his name, therefore, was not unfamiliar to me. In an armchair at the end of the saloon sat Miriam Codd like a small bluebottle, fat and to all appearance friendly. At her right hand, at a little distance, sat the King of Mesopotamia with his doctor. On her left hand at a little distance sat the Coptic Archbishop of Alexandria with his chaplain. Upon his chest flamed a large topaz cross. Mrs. Codd was reading a book with a blue cover. I went boldly towards her and sat down. She said, "Good evening." I said, "Good evening, Mrs. Codd." The Pole had ceased playing and was turning over some music: he wore a fine turquoise ring: the sighing and slapping of the darkened sea reached us through the portholes. I rather hoped that that Pole would start to play again.

Mrs. Codd closed her book, marking the place with a leather marker stamped with the lilies of the Lung' Arno. "Now how," she said, "did you know my name?" "Your name, Mrs. Codd, is written in large white letters on your large black trunks." "Why, so it is. I never thought of that." I failed to understand why this circumstance should have caused her surprise: the trunks, black and shiny, were grouped in the passage: across them, white as the palings of a racing stable, ran the words "Mrs. Miriam Codd," emphatic and indeed assertive, printed in uniform block-capitals. There was a little square box among them which had no space to contain the whole formula: it bore on its lid the large white notice "Codd." It seemed strange to me that the owner of so deliberate a series of inscriptions should have been unaware of the information which they were liable to convey. But in the weeks that followed I was to learn that the infuriating thing about Mrs. Codd was that one could never even approximately foretell by what she would be, or would not be, surprised. Her mind was a calm ocean of indifference punctuated by sporadic reefs.

She smiled at me and asked me my name. If she felt any disappointment she managed to conceal it. "And your hometown?" she added. I was disconcerted by this question and at a loss for the moment how to reply. "Sevenoaks," I answered, accenting the last syllable so as to give to the word a druidic rather than a suburban flavour. "That must be very nice," she commented. I assured her that it was indeed. "And I," she said, "come from Nashville." Seeing no immediate response, she added, "Tennessee." My response at that was immediate. It was evident that we should become fast friends. It was not, at that time, evident how virulent would become our mutual dislike.

I hoped at this stage that she would ask me where I was going. "Well, as a matter of fact," I would have answered, "I am going to Persia." I had found it, in such cases, kinder and more modest to dilute this intoxicating statement with the water of "as a matter of fact": it showed that my journey was not due to any special prowess on my part, but to a coincidence such as might happen to anyone, even to Mrs. Codd. But she did not ask me this question. It was I myself who raised the subject.

"I suppose, Mrs. Codd, that you are going to Luxor?"

"Well, I may do, if I have the time. It must be vurry, vurry interesting."

I advised her that it was certainly not a thing to miss.

"Well, you see, Mr. Nicolson, it's like this. I'm fixed up to go to Persia, and as I'm meeting some friends at Beyrout in January I have to be careful of my dates."

I do not say that I was annoyed by this: I was annoyed only by the way in which she had announced her curious intention. I answered a little vaguely: I said, "Oh, yes—of course." The Pole by then had started to play another tune.

[*3*]

I am not, as I have said, very aware of music, but I can tell when a man plays badly. I have learnt that

mere rapidity of motion or that gambit about crossing the hands are not, as tests of excellence, very reliable: the only sure test for the ignorant is the pianist's treatment of the single note. The bad pianist
will just put one finger on that single note as if indeed it were a simple thing to do: the good pianist,
who, during the involved passages, will have leant
back idly letting his square hands browse miraculously on the key-board, will suddenly be galvanised
into passion at the approach of the single note. His
whole body will become rigid with the intensity of
his concentration: he will lean close down over the
key-board, his trembling forefinger outstretched, and
then he will flick at that note with that forefinger, as
if a dentist extracting a dying nerve. When that happens I fling myself back in my chair. "Dieu," I explain, "comme il joue bien! Quel doigté!"

It happened, at that instant, to the Pole. "Dieu!"
I exclaimed. "God," I corrected, "how well that man
plays! What a touch!" "I don't think he plays very
well," said Mrs. Codd. I didn't expect her to say this,
and I looked up in surprise. "You care very much for
music, Mrs. Codd?" "No, I don't care very much for
music." Again I had drawn a blank. Really this ma-
tronly school-girl was very disconcerting.

"So you are also going to Persia?" I began.

"Why, yes, I'm going to Teeran to stop with Mary
MacCormack."

"I also am going to Tehran."

"Why, fancy that!"

Her voice showed no surprise: it showed no interest. It did not rise a half-note above that flat and
level tone of hers, that tone like a gilt J nib. Again
I felt irritated. The woman was deplorably lacking
in response. Nay! she was lacking in human sympathy. She was not a sympathetic woman. I had been
quite wrong about that lanoline, about that maternal instinct. Mrs. Codd was selfish: Mrs. Codd was a
fool. Had I not sacrificed everything, my comforts,
my home, my family, my friends, in the hope that

this flaming adventure, this ruthless exile, would strip me clean and slim? "Je reviendrai," I had said, "avec des membres de fer, la peau sombre, l'œil furieux: sur mon masque, on me jugera d'une race forte . . . je serai oisif et brutal. Les femmes soignent ces féroces infirmes retournés des pays chauds." This Rimbaud feeling had sustained me during that unpleasant parting at Victoria, it had given me courage when the train slipped through the dusk at Amiens, it had carried me across Paris, it had enabled me to say farewell to Venice without a tear. And now that the ancient parapets of Europe had slipped behind me, already my moral and mental muscles were becoming vigorous and taut. It had been a wrench and an effort to begin this new and exacting chapter: I had with square-jawed defiance turned the page: and there, in the very first paragraph, I had been confronted not by my colleague Sir Richard Burton, but by Miriam Codd.

I looked at her coldly. A plump school-girl nursing a doll. And yet the upper of her two chins had, at moments, a rigid shape about it: there were moments when those eyes ceased to recall Astarte and recalled a garden thistle or even the dark flash of polished steel. It was her voice, her flat and gentle voice, which gave that lanoline effect: it was her figure, her round and lacteal figure, which produced that soothing sense of the maternal. The central core, I reflected, is hard: Miriam Codd is a hard and self-indulgent partridge; Miriam Codd is not an interesting person at all.

"Do you," she was saying to me, "care for ocean voyage?"

"No."

"When did you finish your grade school?"

I was interested by this question, being uncertain both of its meaning and its purpose. But I was anxious not to be drawn into conversation: I was anxious at the moment to manifest displeasure. Above all, as Miriam Codd had shown no interest in my amazing Odyssey, I should show no interest in Miriam Codd. So I answered, "1907." She looked a little surprised at this, but continued her examination.

"I should like to get at your achievement chart. I should like to fix your spare time and recreation record."

"I have no achievements—and but few recreations."

She sighed at this and picked up her book. I glanced at the title. It was *The Golden Bough.*

[4]

After dinner that evening I sat in the saloon reading a really admirable novel by Agatha Christie. I had observed Mrs. Codd on entering, but had avoided her, wishing in the first place to read my book and in the second to evade all further questions about achievement. Colonel Pomeroy was playing bridge exultantly. He flung himself into the game with a proprietary gusto which cast a frightened gloom over his opponents and his partner: Major Tweedie opposite to him would play a card: Colonel Pomeroy would raise his eyebrows in silent endurance: at the end of each rubber the Colonel summarised the play in clipped and masterly phrases which allowed of no appeal. I was sorry for Major Tweedie. The band in the music-room was playing *Tosca.*

I became conscious that someone had sunk very gently into the chair beside me. I glanced up in apprehension of Mrs. Codd: it was only the Pole. His name, I had discovered, was Ostrorog. I returned to Agatha Christie. The Pole interrupted me.

"Vous aimez la musique, Monsieur?"

"Non, je déteste la musique."

"Vous la détestez?"

"Je la déteste."

He laughed a little uncertainly at this, and crossed

his legs. I could see that he was the languid type of invert, whereas the sort I like best are of the brisk variety. So I read my book.

"Vous allez en Perse, Monsieur?"

"Oui, je vais à Téhéran."

"Moi aussi, je vais à Téhéran."

"Vous aussi. . . . ?"

I was appalled. This was really intolerable. I had drawn so vivid a picture of this my Central Asian voyage. The car dashing across the unvintaged desert under alien stars: myself crouching solitary in the back, my hand resting on the leather case of my revolver: that faint dust ahead of us represented the armoured cars: that droning in the air above, the escorting aeroplane: the two dark figures in front— the driver at the wheel, the Iraqi guard with his rifle ready at the knee: the camel-corps lolloping behind. On and on through the night across Arabia: on and on—Jerusalem behind us and in front Baghdad. And my friends that night, dining together at the Ivy, walking back up Shaftesbury Avenue after the theatre. The moon rising as we reached the Euphrates: the dawn upon the Tigris. Saved.

The Colonel had finished his disquisition on the last rubber. "Yes," he was saying, "I try to take a different route each time. Extraordinarily interesting, I can assure you. Extraordinarily interesting. This time it's Jerusalem, Baghdad, Tehran, Meshed, Duzdab, and so to Quetta."

I turned to the Pole. "Le Colonel," I said, "vient avec."

"Ça sera parfait."

I refrained from expressing the full force of my disagreement with that remark. Mrs. Codd, Ostrorog, Colonel Pomeroy! My adventure had ceased to be one. I might as well have remained (I had far better have remained) in Ebury Street. And oh, that pleasant little side-door on the Horse Guards Parade! I had always been opposed to romanticism: one should be more loyal to one's prejudices. I returned to my cabin in a mood of angered remorse.

[5]

The following day we landed at Alexandria. I leant over the side watching the coloured chaos below me, that sudden mutiny in the evening sun. There was Mrs. Codd, a round blue circle, being piloted through the clutching rabble by a uniformed assistant from Shepheard's Hotel. There was Colonel Pomeroy counting his luggage as he had counted the bridge-score, knowing from twenty years' experience how to handle natives. Over there, sitting on a packing-case, was Ostrorog on the verge of tears. Aloof, escorted, privileged, I was the last to descend.

Thereafter followed three helpful days of respite. I went to Cairo and stayed with Charles Hartopp in his flat. I thus avoided meeting my future companions. On the fourth day I left for Jerusalem. I knew they were in the train, but was able to evade them. The train stopped at El Kantara, where there is a ferry which takes one across the Suez Canal. In the dark it did not look in the least like a canal; one had no impression of the rectilinear; it looked like some small harbour where great steamers congregate, like Queenstown in the old days, like Newhaven, like the Hook of Holland. White mast-lights high up among the stars, red lights low-clustering by the water, one arc-light illuminating a row of trucks. Across the harbour shone the windows of the *wagon-lit*. The ferry itself was bright and garish, like a tram or a houseboat: there was a white garden seat newly painted. I got there first: the other three joined me in succession: Mrs. Codd, gentle and uninterested: Colonel Pomeroy, flustered and managing: Ostrorog, battered and perturbed. The ferry gave a sudden hoot like a launch and the surrounding lights began to sway across each other as we slowly moved. We were leaving Africa: we were going to Asia. "How strange," I said to Mrs. Codd, "that two such unwieldy continents should be so contiguous!" She said, "Yes, indeed!" I felt my remark was worthy of a more enlightened reception. "Etrange," I said to Ostrorog, "que deux continents aussi difformes et maladroits soient si contigus." "Parfaitement," he answered, "Monsieur." I was disheartened by this and did not try my apophthegm upon the Colonel. The ferry, on reaching Asia, bumped delicately against the quay.

Our luggage was deposited in the long brown body of the sleeping-car: we waited in the station buffet upon a little terrace looking back over the canal. Ostrorog had a glass of Benedictine and then two more: Mrs. Codd ordered tea: the Colonel had a whisky-and-soda: I had a glass of tepid beer. The trucks over there in Africa clanked backwards and forwards under the now distant arc-light: the little electric bulb above us, pendant and naked on its cord, showed red against the diamond white of stars. "Oh," I murmured, "le crépuscule des petits ports."

"Plaît-il?" Ostrorog inquired.

I did not repeat my remark. I was listening to the Colonel and Mrs. Codd. "Well," he was saying, exultant again and breathless. "And so here we are! Extraordinarily interesting. And to-morrow we shall wake up in Palestine. Ever been to Palestine, Mrs. Codd?"

"I have never been to Palestine, Colonel Pomeroy."

"Disappointing, of course, at first sight. But extraordinarily interesting for all that. Jerusalem, you know. It gives one a feeling of emotion in spite of oneself."

"Yes," said Mrs. Codd, "it may do. A strong conditioned stimulus (because, as I always say, a stimulus can be vurry intensely conditioned), a vurry, vurry strong conditioned response."

The Colonel blinked at this considerably. I leant forward with an awakened interest. "So you also," I said, "are a behaviourist?"

Mrs. Codd assumed a new dignity. Her eyes peered out across the gentle canal, looking westwards. "I am an experimenter," she said slowly, "at the Harriet Putzheim Medical School."

And so this was the explanation! That indifference to all experience and association: that placidity: that apparent stupidity: that evident cunning: that soft firmness: that motherly look, and again that flash of cruelty. An experimenter at the Harriet Putzheim Medical School! I knew something about the Harriet Putzheim. It is where they take little children and prove to themselves that the only inherent instinct is that of fear produced by either (a) noise, or (b) bumps. Little Leah aged eighteen months is given a frog one morning instead of her bottle: she shows no surprise: but on the third morning an experimenter stands behind and when the frog is produced the experimenter utters a loud yell close to Leah's ear: thereafter Leah does not care for frogs. Little Ikey, again, aged fifteen months, is allowed to play with a rabbit: on the fourth day, when the rabbit is produced, Ikey is sharply bumped by the experimenter upon the floor: this produces a conditioned response: the bumping process is called "loss of support": thereafter, when the rabbit is produced, Ikey screams. It is all very interesting and conclusive: the experimenters, on their charts, register with hard and competent eyes a further triumph over Mr. William James.

I looked at Mrs. Codd with a cold surmise. I was a little shocked. I glanced at Colonel Pomeroy and saw that he was more than a little shocked. I leant towards him:—"Mrs. Codd," I said, "is a behaviourist." I accented the first four syllables of the word, since I feared that he had mistaken the lady's profession. I think he was reassured. He murmured, "Extraordinarily interesting," and began to chink some money against his glass to bring the waiter. I turned to Ostrorog: "Madame," I said to him, "est une conduitiste." "Plaît-il?" he said. "Une conduitiste," I repeated firmly: from Ostrorog at least I would stand no nonsense. Mrs. Codd sat there placidly, not displeased with the effect of her disclosure. Suddenly the engine behind us gashed the gentle night with a shriek of impatience: Mrs. Codd jumped in her chair and gave a little scream. "Noise?" I said to her. The waiter was clearing the table: he pushed her chair: she flamed at him a look of fury: "Loss of support?" I asked her. She did not answer these questions. It was from that moment, I think, that she began intensely to dislike me.

We climbed into our sleeping-cars and left for Jerusalem.

[6]

Three nights later, two dusted Cadillacs of the Nairn Transport Company swung under the Jaffa Gate and drew up in front of the Allenby Hotel. The first car was fully occupied by a Syrian family: in the second car there were places for Colonel Pomeroy, Count Ostrorog, myself and Miriam Codd. For the latter's insistent luggage, as I immediately pointed out, there was no room at all. I got them to rope my own luggage on to the splash-boards while the others were at dinner. We were to start at 9 P.M. Having completed my preparations I entered the hotel and passed along the corridor to the dining-room. The Syrian family were having a large meal in the corner on the left: in the corner on the right sat Colonel Pomeroy, Count Ostrorog and Miriam Codd. The Colonel was doing host: "Now what about some more bread—what? Waiter! Some more bread!"

I sat down at a little table in the centre of the room next to the one occupied by the Nairn drivers. Two tired young men they were, with bloodshot eyes and eyebrows white with the dust of the road from Haifa. I asked them when we should reach

Baghdad. They had no idea. One could never cal-
culate on the Ammon route, something was almost
certain to happen. We must trust to luck. I groaned
at the prospect of motoring with Colonel Pomeroy
for seven days trusting to luck. Three days and
nights to Baghdad, four days on to Tehran. Would
it really take us three whole days of constant motion
to reach Baghdad? They hoped not, it had been done
in two. They were polite but tired: they answered
my questions as a Channel steward answers when
asked whether it is going to be rough.

I had been very nimble during those three days
at Jerusalem in evading my companions. I had not
stayed at the hotel: I had stayed with Ronald Storrs
—paragon among hosts, paragon among cicerones.
I asked him about Mrs. Codd. "Oh, my God," he
said, "not *that* woman!" So thenceforward I had an
ally in my campaign of evasion. We managed it
beautifully: we had seen them bearing down upon
us across the wide terrace of the Mosque of Omar,
and had escaped by jumping down a wall: on the
next day Mrs. Codd had been observed and avoided
in the vicinity of Bethlehem: that very morning, on
hearing the words "extraordinarily interesting," I
had dodged behind the Holy Sepulchre. As I sat
there in the dining-room of the Allenby Hotel I realised that my hours of liberty were drawing to a
close. One of the drivers glanced at his watch and
made a sign to his companion. They left the room
and the Syrian family scuttled out after them. Colonel Pomeroy rose and put on a dust-coat and a solar
topee: he sucked his teeth and wriggled into a pair
of field-glasses on a long strap: again he sucked his
teeth and wriggled with the other arm under the
strap of a long leather-covered flask. As they passed
my table the Colonel said "En route" to me, heart-
ily. I ordered a liqueur-brandy. I felt that I did not
want that evening to cross Arabia in the least.

It was 10 P. M. before we started. The cars under

the street lamps bulged with packages enclosed in nets. They looked like two large and dusty widows returning from market. A few idlers hung around us, a few Palestinian idlers: for three days we should not see strangers again, for three days I should see only the familiar faces of my present companions: I looked wistfully at the porter of the Allenby Hotel: what a gulf, I felt, separated him from his colleague at Baghdad. I leant forward and lovingly pressed a note into his hand. It was my farewell to humanity. The car hooted at that, and then jerked off and out under the Damascus Gate: it then swerved to the right, past the Gate of Herod and the Tower of the Storks. The great walls loomed square above us against the stars. We began to descend: a few olive trees flashed into the circle of the headlights and flicked back again into the dark: a village street illumined suddenly, an open door showing a deal table and a lamp, the hurried barking of dogs. "Bethany," I murmured. "Now was that really Bethany?" exclaimed the Colonel. "How extraordinarily interesting!" I decided not to speak again. For an hour we descended in and out of hair-pin bends, and as we dropped into the valley the night-air softened and we missed the scent of thyme. Some lights to the left there clustered below us. "Jericho," I thought, but I did not say so. The Colonel and Mrs. Codd in the back seat were silent and perhaps asleep. Ostrorog and I sat loosely in the two middle seats that folded up. They were not uncomfortable. We stopped when we reached the Jordan, and our passports were examined: to the right and left of us shrilled the high note of frogs. It was after midnight when we reached Rabboth Ammon.

There were some tents there under the high embankment of the Hedjaz railway, and we had some sardines and tea: Mrs. Codd was given a tent to herself and left us: the Colonel, Ostrorog and I slept on mattresses where we were: the Syrian family slept in their car: the moon rose, and with it the dogs of Rab-both Ammon began to bark: a goods train clattered in from Aleppo. I cannot say that I slept well.

It was still dark when they aroused us and we bun-dled sleepily into our car by the light of a single lantern. The dawn broke grey and bitter as we left the hills. The Colonel, thank God, and Mrs. Codd were both asleep. Their heads jerked and swayed as the car swung on, over the hillocks of tufted lava, over the banks of shale. It was very cold. The sun climbed up behind some black volcanic mountains: it swept gaily over that barren landscape: it touched with gold the dust-cloud behind us: it touched with gold the face of Mrs. Codd. She awoke.

"My!" she exclaimed, "it isn't flat."

"No, Mrs. Codd, the Arabian desert is not flat. It is, in fact, intersected by mountains."

"And it isn't sandy."

"In the Nefud Roala to the south of us, you have red sand. The northern portion which we are about to enter is composed, however, of aluminous silicates. We shall reach the sandy portion after we have passed the Jebel Anaize."

The driver spoke to me over his shoulder. "We don't pass the Jebel Anaize: we go south by the Wad el Tebel. We shall get stuck there, unless we're lucky, in the mud."

"The North Arabian desert," I explained to Mrs. Codd, "known locally as El Hamad, is comparatively well watered. We may get bogged."

Mrs. Codd had closed her eyes again and pre-tended to be asleep. It was possible that she did not care for information. The Colonel, whose head swayed with open mouth, undoubtedly was asleep. Ostrorog sat pale and silent: a faint red bristle had grown upon his chin. We pursued our way across Arabia.

[7]

The morning sun blazed straight in front of us: we were travelling east. At nine o'clock we stopped for breakfast: we gathered camel-thorn and lit a bonfire: at one edge of the bonfire we tilted the kettle, at the other a tin of sausages. The driver produced little cardboard cups and plates: on the front of the plates was printed "Trans desert mail: Nairn Transport Company": on the back of the plates, the legend, "If you have complaints, tell us: if you have no complaints, tell your friends." I was pleased by this tactful little message from the brothers Nairn, and my respect for their efficiency, already great, was much increased. The Colonel for his part was by now thoroughly awake: he fussed about laying the breakfast, counting one, two, three, four. "And, by Jove," he said, "marmalade! They do one well and no mistake." Mrs. Codd, in a motherly way and in very elementary French, was having a confidential conversation with the Pole. I sat and read the *Anabasis* of Xenophon in the Loeb edition: I read the English side of the page, but when I came to a point of interest it was the Greek side that I marked. The kettle, after a while, began to boil: the sausages were emptied from their tin: the Colonel was again becoming exultant. Ostrorog had been pouring into the ears of Miriam Codd the secrets of what I fear must have been a troubled and an epicene past. She nodded her head from time to time and said, "Je vois": there was a firm look in her round little face: the mother was rapidly being lost in the experimenter. We had breakfast. The Colonel, with old-world courtesy, acted as host.

I was assailed by two preoccupations: (1) Would the Colonel begin talking when we started again? Would he go on talking till we reached Baghdad? I apprehended stories of other deserts: of the Dasht-i-

Lut, of Takla Makan, of the sandy desert of Kizil-Kum. All this would encourage Mrs. Codd to speak of Arizona, and Ostrorog to talk to us about the Steppes. It was a gloomy prospect. (2) My second pre-occupation was of a more kindly nature. I was worried about Mrs. Codd and her managements. Surely it would be very difficult for a lady in Arabia, with no cloakroom handy, and four men there, and no cover? But my preoccupation on these two points was unnecessary. The first was solved by Mrs. Codd saying as she helped herself to butter: "Let's get our conversation over now: we mustn't talk in the motor." The second was solved, a few minutes later, by her just walking off. A round blue figure stumping off solitary in the direction of Medina: a round blue figure returning to us from the south.

And on we went. The sun was above us. The sun sank behind. Towards evening three vultures scattered at our passage: they flapped off languidly with trailing feet, and settled again some fifteen yards away: the body of an Arab lay there with the guts exposed: he was the first human being we had seen for four hundred miles. Mrs. Codd glanced at him indifferently, as if at a cinema poster passed at Purley. The Colonel said, "My God! Did you see that?" Ostrorog, under his pink incipient beard, turned a paler shade of green. The sun sank with a bump behind a black range of volcanic mountains. In forty minutes the stars were strewn above us like grains of scattered rice.

I was awakened five hours later by the sudden jerk of stoppage. In front of us, close against the blaze of our headlights, appeared an object of amazing fantasy: a jumbled mass of fresh white wood and fresh white canvas torn and shattered to a height of fifteen feet. Here and there among the wreckage glittered a strand of aluminium, or the torpedo-heads of aluminium cylinders. It appeared like some vast toy, some vast consignment of elaborate toys, smashed upon arrival. The driver turned back into the recesses of the car. "This," he said, "is where Maitland crashed. We have come along fine. We should make Baghdad to-morrow. Supper now."

We tore the canvas and the woodwork from the lonely aeroplane: a great flame leapt up and licked the darkness: we sat beside it: the kettle and the sausages were tucked into the corners: more cardboard plates were produced. Mrs. Codd had pins and needles: she sank down on an air-cushion and stretched her little buttoned feet in front of her, gyrating the toe-caps. "That," I suggested, "is what you call the Babinski reflex." She looked at me with eyes expressive (there was no doubt about it) of hatred. It was evident that she imagined I was making a mock of behaviourism, that I was making a mock of Miriam Codd. In this, to a large extent, she was mistaken. For I had heard Mr. Sebastian Sprott in London state that behaviourism was not in itself ridiculous: and what Sprott says, I believe. But none the less she turned her round blue back on me and continued her intent examination of the conditioned responses of Count Ostrorog. I felt that I could have told her quite quickly what was wrong with the Pole: her scant knowledge of the French language rendered her experimentation unnecessarily complicated. But I was not the one to assist unasked. I also turned my back and faced the Colonel. The latter, thank God, was very tired indeed: he drank his flask in silence: he gazed hard at a sardine tin: "Extraordinarily interesting," he murmured, but, as it were, to himself. The Syrian party had long since disappeared.

I ate in silence, gazing into the red heart of the flames. I was perfectly aware that around me stretched Arabia Deserta: that beside me, a point of civilisation in a radius of several hundred miles, were grouped a Cadillac, an English driver, a behaviourist, a Colonel, a smashed aeroplane, a Polish neuropath, some sausages, tea, cardboard plates, marmalade, Lea and Perrin's sauce. These facts grouped themselves in the peripheral focus: my attention was concentrated upon the conversation, the very curious conversation taking place between the Count and Miriam Codd. She was getting into very deep water; it had been some time since he, for his part, had felt the slightest touch of ground beneath his feet.

"Non," she was saying, "pas complex. Habites. Coutumes."

"Plaît-il?" repeated Ostrorog, a little wearily.

Mrs. Codd was becoming impatient. It was inevitable that sooner or later she should pocket her pride.

"Mr. Nicolson," she said at last, "what is the French for 'congestion of the pituitary gland'?"

"Congestion," I answered, "de la glande pituitaire."

"Plaît-il?" said Ostrorog.

"You better just try 'pituite.'"

"Pituite," chirped Miriam Codd.

"Plaît-il?" said the Pole.

"Would you explain to the Count that the unconscious is not a sex repression but an unverbalised glandular habit?"

"Madame veut dire que l'inconscient ne dérive pas de la suppression de l'instinct sexuel, mais qu'il n'est en effet qu'une habitude glandulaire non-verbalisée."

"Plaît-il?"

"And what does one say for untrained visceral organisation?"

"Mal au cœur."

"You know very well," she said sharply, "that I am not referring merely to alimentary trouble."

"Well, I should try 'indiscipline viscérale.'"

She tried it, but it had no success. She gave me up for a bit, but collapsed again in front of "unstriped muscular habit." "Une habitude," I said (and after all why shouldn't I?), "des muscles non-bariolés, des muscles, c'est-à-dire, qui ne sont pas à raies."

"Plaît-il?"

Mrs. Codd turned to me indignantly: "You don't

help one bit, Mr. Nicolson. I really think you might assist."

"But you see, Mrs. Codd . . . You see—well, hadn't we better leave it for the moment?"

It was a relief when we were herded again into the motor. The driver was tying the kettle on to the splash-board. "You see," said Mrs. Codd, a note of despair rasping in her voice, "he believes in *congenital* degeneracy. I can't convince him that heredity, if it exists at all, is merely intra-uterine behaviour. I may not have made it quite clear. Mr. Nicolson, you might just explain to him before we start."

I was firm about this. After all we had had a tiring day. We had had two tiring days. "No," I said, "Mrs. Codd, I will not."

The cranking of the engine interfered with her reply.

[*8*]

A second dawn glimmered in front of us: the sun this time rose from a sweep of rolling sand-hills. We breasted them, and dipped over the edge. In the valley thus disclosed were two armoured cars: there was a little pool beyond with some English soldiers bathing: their knees and forearms showed like burnt umber against the white of their thighs. They ran a little way towards us, and cheered, waving their topees above their tousled heads. They had little sense of decency. Mrs. Codd put on her Harriet Putzheim expression: the Colonel clambered out. A sergeant appeared hurriedly from behind one of the cars, his chin lathered, a shaving-brush in his hand. He waved the brush with a welcoming gesture at the advancing Colonel. The latter held a brisk and friendly inspection: he returned to us aglow with satisfaction. "Fine boys, fine boys: based on Ramadieh: fine set of fellows." He hummed to himself and smacked his lips. "Fancy shaving like that, two hundred miles from nowhere! Good show that. First-class show." I also had experienced a slight tremor of that Kipling feeling. For the first time I felt a certain kinship with the Colonel. "Ramadieh, did you say, sir?" I put in the "sir" because of my Kipling feeling. Also because I knew it would annoy Mrs. Codd. It did. Ostrorog for his part was too exhausted to observe or comprehend.

At midday we crossed the Euphrates: we spun over the waste of hardened sand which separates the two rivers: a mirage danced in front of us, trees and water and cool marine caves. At five o'clock a fringe of palm trees edged the distance, and above them a single factory chimney belching smoke. The sun was setting as we crossed the Tigris and lurched into Baghdad.

They told us that a convoy was starting for Persia the next morning: we could take the train that night, and at dawn we would find the cars waiting for us at Khanikin. We were too dazed by then to question: like sheep we gathered for dinner in the Maude Hotel: like sheep we drove to the station: like sheep we huddled silent and exhausted in the railway carriage. It was a long saloon with slatted window-blinds and two large horse-hair settees. We lay there dusty and unshaven, our heads propped upon our luggage. Ostrorog looked seriously ill: the Colonel had finally lost his commanding manner: Miriam Codd alone remained the same. I dozed fitfully as the train dragged its cautious way towards the frontier.

The third aching dawn found us on the platform at Khanikin. Such sleep as we had snatched during the night had restored, to some degree, our powers of self-assertion. It had not restored our nerves. We had some breakfast at the canteen, sitting opposite to each other in silent hostility. I looked at the Colonel, I looked at Mrs. Codd, I looked at Ostrorog. No—one thing at least was certain: it was certain that I could not endure, I could not possibly endure, another four days in such a company. Mrs. Codd with a meditative but determined expression looked at me. A hard and a cruel look steeled itself in her eyes. She rose firmly and approached the station-master.

"Could you tell me, please, when I could get a train back to Baghdad?" He did not understand English and summoned a man who did. She would have to wait for the day, but could take the same train back at midnight. She walked back to us, with a return of that azure gentleness which had so misled me that afternoon on the *Helouan*. "I have rather a headache," she said, "I don't think I shall come on to Persia after all." The Colonel expressed regret: "Very sorry, upon my word." I said nothing. And Ostrorog for his part had failed to understand.

The cars by that time had arrived. There was a little Dodge limousine like a taxi. There was a high Fiat lorry for the baggage. I dashed to the lorry and climbed without a word beside the driver's seat. The Colonel and Ostrorog disappeared into the Dodge. Mrs. Codd came in front of the station to see us start. The road beyond us was a sea of viscous mud. We splashed across it for a hundred yards and then the limousine stuck, its wheels revolving helplessly. My own lorry dashed onwards to the corner there by the palm grove. Across the road, in front of me, down from the hill, ran a fence of posts and wire ending in a gate and guard-house with a green and white flag. That gate was the gate to Persia. I looked round. Mrs. Codd, a blue circle, was waving from the station, she was waving a white handkerchief. Again, thus haloed by distance and farewell, she seemed small and gentle and friendly. The limousine was still embedded in the slime. From its window emerged the solar topee of Colonel Pomeroy. My heart sang with liberation. I leant out and backwards beyond the body of the van. I took off my hat: I waved it triumphantly at Colonel Pomeroy: I waved it at the diminishing blue bubble of Mrs. Codd. A few minutes later I entered Persia. And alone.

Sir Harold Nicolson was born in Teheran in 1886. After his graduation from Balliol College, Oxford, he entered the British foreign service, and from 1909 to 1929 held diplomatic posts in Madrid, Istanbul, Teheran and Berlin. From 1935 to 1945 he was a member of Parliament. During his active career he wrote 35 books of history, biography and fiction. Some of his chief works are *Tennyson* (1923), *Some People* (1927), *Lord Carnock* (1930), *Public Faces* (1932), *Peacemaking* (1933), *Dwight Morrow* (1935), *The Congress of Vienna* (1946), *King George V: His Life and Reign* (1952), *Journey to Java* (1957) and *Monarchy* (1962). He contributed to British, American and European journals all his life. His most famous series of articles, "Marginal Comment," ran in the *Spectator* from 1938 to 1952. He died in 1968.